HOW TO WRITE
SIMPLE AND EFFECTIVE
SMALL WORKS CONTRACTS
IN JUST

500
WORDS

Dedication

To Lorna McCallum and Rowena Birch
who challenge me to be the best I can.

HOW TO WRITE SIMPLE AND EFFECTIVE SMALL WORKS CONTRACTS IN JUST 500 WORDS

SARAH FOX

First published in Great Britain in 2020

Published by
500 Words Ltd
Ash Cottage
Hawthorn Lane
Wilmslow
Cheshire
SK9 5DG

A catalogue record for this book is available from the British Library.

ISBN: 978-0-9955409-5-8

Book design and typesetting by Ashdown Creative
www.ashdowncreative.co.uk

Cover photograph © Adobe Stock

CONTENTS

FOREWORD

I was surprised on my first working visit to Japan to find that the contract for a massive new building in Shinjuku was written on one page. The reason that was possible is the subject of another essay. But it gives context to Sarah Fox's long quest to simplify and compress the language of UK contract writing. This book is its natural outcome: a small works contract writing guide. When the works are small, surely so can be the contract? This is not a template or standard form to edit but a writer's guide to putting an agreement together that covers all the bases.

It is written primarily for builders seeking to offer a contract to their customer. That customer may often be a consumer rather than a business and thus subject to the protections provided to consumers who cannot be expected to have equal awareness of the issues and conventions of contractual relationships. They may or may not have professional advisers.

Many customers and builders are lax in matters of contract, setting off too soon, failing to agree clear requirements or changing their minds. Sarah provides a five-part guide, setting down in twenty-four short chapters why the contract should be a simple one, how you can write the minimum, how to make it client-centric, how to ensure contract terms are legally effective and the final steps to success.

The central challenge in winning work and making a success of it is to be able to define the client's requirements clearly and to communicate well and continuously with the customer. The contract should capture that scope of work and the terms under which it will be delivered, including quality, time, cost and payment. The project plan of work is a natural companion to the contract, and both should, in Sarah's view, be one-pagers, readily on view, pinned to the office notice board or on the tablet screen. It is no use to put them in a drawer. 'Plan the Work and Work to the Plan' was a mantra in my early career at BDP.

This book will help not only small works builders and their customers but also those working at any scale: clients, advisers, designers and constructors. It boils away the verbiage to concentrate on essentials for users, not for their lawyers. It's about a relationship at heart, between buyer and seller. The Japanese one-pager is the product of relationships between the client and contractor firms which may go back centuries and involve cross-ownerships right down the supply chain. Nobody lets anyone down in such circumstances. The least we can do here is to be clear, concise and trustworthy.

Sarah can be forgiven for one idiosyncrasy. In a world of contracts written as if all parties were men, she assumes in her book that the customer is a woman. Other contracts, like JCT, may be going 'gender neutral', but meanwhile we can enjoy the counterbalance.

Richard Saxon CBE is chairman of JCT, the contract-writing body. He is also a client adviser and a champion of construction industry modernisation. Formerly he was chairman of BDP, the international design consultancy, a vice-president of RIBA and a founder and president of the British Council for Offices. www.saxoncbe.com

INTRODUCTION

Small works projects need short robust contracts. Makes sense, right? Large and complex projects have a plentiful supply of contracts to choose from, but the choices for small works projects are very limited. You might take one of the monster standard forms (you may even try to cut it down to size); or you might copy and paste random content off the Internet; you could spend a few pounds downloading a contract off a contract website and hope it does the trick; or you might keep your fingers crossed that a proposal plus a hefty dollop of trust is *good enough*.

Rather than telling you that you cannot write your own contract or you must use someone else's 'standard' contract, this book takes a different approach: it will act as your guide to writing a small works contract that is crystal clear, safeguards your business and will not annoy your clients.

In just a few pages you will learn the bare minimum your contract needs, how to add four items to make it client-centred, and how to expand the content to make it effective and workable. You will be sure what you can and cannot do, when you have promised that the works will be completed, how the original contract details can be changed as the project progresses and how much you will get paid.

Why Contracts for Small Works?

Small works contracts, like all legal agreements, are tools to *help you do business*. Like any tool in your business tool box, it should be fit for its intended purpose, and used in the right way.

Although there are over 150 standard form contracts in the UK construction industry, from more than 10 different publishers, only three focus on projects for small works. That's 2% of the published content to serve the needs of the nearly half a million people engaged in construction projects who are SMEs, sole traders, jobbing builders, entrepreneurs and micro-enterprises.

Most of these companies and businesses do not have internal legal assistance and may struggle to adapt, complete and negotiate the existing standard forms (or even to choose between them). Although the Joint Contracts Tribunal (JCT) Home Owner Contract has been awarded the crystal mark by the Plain English campaign, that accreditation is no guarantee that the contract is easy to read, understand and use (see below).

My 25-year experience with standard form contracts is that they are designed not for users, but for lawyers. This book shares what I've learnt working with hundreds of businesses from trade associations to one-woman bands to help you write better contracts and use them successfully.

Why 500 Words?

Unlike its longer cousins, a 500-word small works contract positively encourages you to get your contract signed *before* you start work. Roughly one-third of UK construction projects start without a contract being in place. With a contract that is much quicker to read, understand, negotiate and finalise, you minimise the risk that quibbling over words or clauses will delay getting your contract agreed and signed.

In 2012, my twin sister challenged me to write a construction contract in just 500 words: that's a single A4 page. I started from scratch and created a contract that is simple, uncluttered, easy to use, and legally robust. That first contract led onto a series of construction agreements, including a letter of intent, appointment, collateral warranty and the small works contract.

In 2017, I was commissioned by the Federation of Master Builders (FMB), one of the UK's largest trade associations, to rewrite their contracts for their members. We created a short form contract as well as simplifying their domestic and commercial contracts. We knew that builders presented with long contracts – with checklists, boxes and optional clauses to fill in, cross out or tick off – were simply not using them. Although the Plain English Campaign had awarded its crystal mark to the FMB's previous contracts, the documents were too long, overly complex and not user-friendly. Since their re-launch in 2018, member usage has nearly doubled with 8,000 downloads in a year.

This book explains how you can write simple and effective small works contracts. You can write contracts which safeguard your business without annoying your clients. This book will also persuade you to go against the conventional wisdom that length is good by explaining why a 500-word contract is better.

Who Should Read This Book?

This book is written for:

- Builders, contractors and tradespeople who are trying to run their own micro-enterprise or small business and would like something better than copy and pasting random terms off the Internet

- Procurement staff, managers, lawyers, your in-house 'contracts expert' and anyone who writes or reviews small works contracts

- Advisors who want to understand and explain the content and pitfalls of using the monster standard form contracts.

This book focuses on contractors working in the UK construction industry, although the overall messages and direction translate into other industries, countries and specialisms.

Once you have met a prospective client, and that client believes you have the expertise to meet her* needs, you need to persuade her to use you as her contractor. This requires both client-specific information (often in a proposal or quote) and a set of more generic terms and conditions. Together they record your agreement for this client and this project.

---

*Although companies are gender neutral, many small works contracts are with individuals. I have chosen 'she/her' to represent the client partly to redress the balance with the ubiquitous use of 'he/him'. Neither discrimination nor stereotyping is intended.

Your documents need to clearly demonstrate to your client that you understand her needs, are competent and trustworthy, and what she can expect when you work together. For small works contracts, your client may never have been involved in a construction project before so you also need to deal with some of the myths she believes and manage her expectations of the process. You need to make sure your contract is legally robust and effective – one that both of you can *read, understand and use.*

The Structure

After explaining what a small works contract is, this book is presented in five parts:

Part A: Why you should write simple small works contracts. Long construction contracts are the norm in the UK construction industry, so this Part highlights the benefits of shorter, more readable, more usable contracts. It explains the five legal requirements you need for your small works contract to be legally binding, and why you should use a simple contract.

Part B: How you can write the bare minimum. This sets out, step-by-step, the bare minimum your small works contract needs to be legally binding – at the end of this Part your contract will be sufficient but neither client-specific nor effective. It also explains some basic principles of writing agreements of any sort.

Part C: How you can write client-centred content. This sets out the four elements your small works contract must have to reflect the needs of your client. It takes you step-by-step through how to avoid common errors, what happens if you add nothing to your contract, then why and how you can write it simply.

Part D: How you can write effective small works contracts. This introduces effective extras which help you to create a workable small works contract. It takes the same step-by-step approach as Parts B and C.

Part E: Next steps for contract success. This summarises how to use your small works contract successfully. It helps you to ask better questions before you send it and provides a Happiness Check to ensure your clients are as impressed with your contract as you are.

The chapters are presented in 500-word blocks, to show that even complex legal issues do not require long-winded explanations. As that is true of legal issues, you will realise how much easier it can be to describe your client's small works project in just 500 words.

In this book, 'you' refers to the builder. However in the contract clauses – the sample text you can adopt and use in your small works contract – I have used a conversational style. So the contractor is referred to as 'we/our' and the client as 'you/your'. For example, instead of 'The Builder will' my small works contract uses 'We will'. Other ideas for improving the readability of your contracts can be found in the International Association for Contract and Commercial Management (IACCM) contract design pattern library.[1]

How To Read This Book

The book is short, so it won't take you long to read. You should read it from start to finish, and mark sections which you know you'll want to return to before you start your next project. By applying its tips, you will create a small works contract that is simple, uncluttered, easy to use, and legally robust.

500 words refers to the contract template. How you define the scope of your works, the payment schedule, quality descriptions and other project-specific data will take you above the word count.

This book reflects the laws of England and Wales (although I will refer to English law to cover both). As a user guide, this book is not a comprehensive explanation of all the relevant cases or statutes, nor is it a substitute for legal advice. Depending on your previous experience, you may want to get your lawyer to review whether your content is a good fit for your client and her project.

1

WHAT IS A SMALL WORKS CONTRACT?

A small works contract is a simplified, short form, construction contract for smaller projects.

In the UK construction industry there are a number of standard form contracts for simple projects, including ones from trade associations like the Federation of Master Builders, professional bodies like Royal Institute of British Architects, or from cross-sector publishers like the Joint Contracts Tribunal. Each of these has its fans and its critics.

Using these forms is undoubtedly quicker than writing your own, but their terms and processes may not suit the way you do business or – and this is their greatest failing – their content may not be easy to read, understand and use by an ordinary member of the public. Using those contracts for small works projects may not serve the needs of your clients.

A small works contract covers everything from a 1-page handwritten estimate confirming the price and works, across a wide spectrum to a 50-page all-singing all-dancing contract. At its core is a contract that says:

■ the *Client* must provide access, information, approvals and pay for the works being carried out at her home (or other property)

◼ the *Contractor* agrees to carry out a specified schedule of works, for an agreed price and to an agreed quality standard and within a (proposed) timescale.

A Small Works Contract Helps You Do Business

As with other legally binding agreements (aka contracts), the purpose of a small works contract is to *help you to do business*. It should help you safeguard your business *without* annoying your clients.

As a tool to *help you do business*, your small works contract should clearly record what each party has agreed. This prevents misunderstandings, and means the contract acts as a guide to what you (and your client) need to do. This type of contract will also help you avoid disputes.

A Small Works Contract is (Sometimes) a Construction Contract

Any contract for the carrying out of works on a project in the UK may be a 'construction contract'[2] as defined by UK legislation; i.e. an agreement recording the details of works, installation of materials, or services to be provided for a building, development or construction project. The exceptions relevant to small works contracts are that it is not a construction contract if (1) it is works on your client's home, or (2) the works will take less than 45 days.

If it is a construction contract, it needs to meet certain minimum requirements on payment [Chapter 11].

A Small Works Contract is (Sometimes) a Consumer Contract

If your project is for works on a client's home, then your small works contract will be subject to the Consumer Rights Act 2015.[3] Terms will be implied into your small works contract if you don't make an alternative provision. These terms cover time, cost and quality as well as the binding nature of information on which your client relies. The Act also provides remedies for consumers if the works do not meet the criteria set out in the Act. [Chapter 17]

2

TEN FREQUENTLY ASKED QUESTIONS

1. **When should I use a small works contract?** The simple answer is when you think your client's project is small works. That depends on the complexity of the design or works, the client, the client's needs, the risks relating to the project, and your own experience. Price is not the only factor.

2. **What can I include in my small works contract?** Under English law, the parties have freedom to contract, which means you can include anything you like provided you meet the five requirements for a contract. [Chapter 3]

3. **What's wrong with standard forms?** The standard form contracts for small or minor works tend to assume a sophisticated client with a good understanding of construction and legal jargon. Your clients may not fit those assumptions.

4. **Can I avoid contracts?** You *could* carry out small works projects using only a quote as it probably covers the bare minimum [Part B]. However your quote may not cover the client-centred content or the effective extras [Parts C and D] which manage the project and build trust. Without *any* paperwork, you may not even have a right to finish the project; if you do finish you *should* get paid, but you may have to rely on a judge to tell you how much.

5. **How can I ensure I get paid?** Nothing you write into your small works contract will *guarantee* that your client will pay for your goods, works and services. It's better to check if your client has the financial resources to meet your agreed price and any wider costs she will incur on the project *before* you sign (or e-sign) on the dotted line. However, your small works contract can include terms to encourage regular payments [Chapter 11] and discourage late payments. [Chapter 17]

6. **How can I write a watertight small works contract?** You can't.

7. **Why do disputes happen?** According to the 2019 Arcadis Global Disputes Report[4], the top cause of global disputes is users failing to understand or use their construction contracts. This is more likely when contracts are too long, overly complex, and not user-friendly.

8. **What can be done to minimise the risk of disputes?** As well as simple effective terms, frequent communication with your client is critical to managing her expectations, ensuring she understands how her project is progressing and keeping her updated on any changes. Ask her to complete the Happiness Check. [Chapter 23]

9. **What's the main risk in *writing* a small works contract?** The main risk in writing a small works contract is that you do not spell out clearly enough what your client needs to pay and when, and how the project may change and evolve.

10. **What's the main risk in *using* a small works contract?** The main risk is that you shove it in a drawer (or file electronically) and never re-read it. You may forget what you have agreed to provide, and you won't remind your client about her duties.

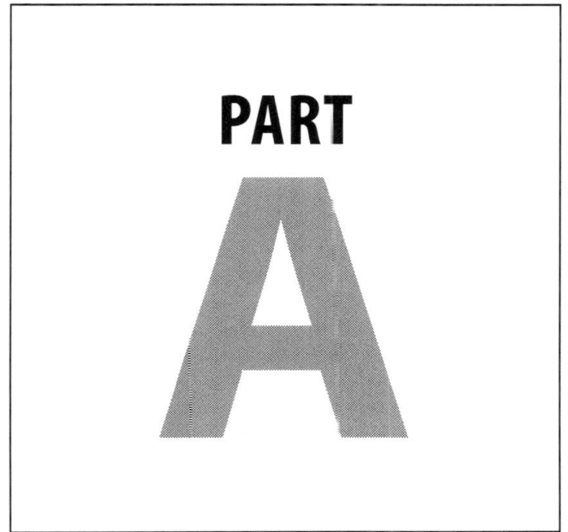

WHY YOU SHOULD WRITE SIMPLE SMALL WORKS CONTRACTS

This Part explores what you need for a contract and considers three key reasons to write simple small works contracts:

1. **To give your client confidence.** One-third of UK construction projects[5] begin without *any* form of contract. If you want to start professionally, then you need to write a simple contract that does not annoy your client. This will give your client confidence in your competence. [Chapter 4]

2. **To safeguard your business.** The most effective way to safeguard your business is to limit your liability, while at the same time providing a clear record of what you and your client have agreed. [Chapter 5]

3. **To avoid disputes.** If you want to avoid disputes, you should write a small works contract that you and your client can easily read, understand and use. [Chapter 6]

By the end of this Part, you should be convinced to write a simple small works contract.

3

WHAT IS A CONTRACT?

A contract is a legally binding agreement; a promise that can be relied on and enforced. It doesn't need any specific form, words or style. It doesn't even need to be written down.

To be legally binding, your small works contract has to satisfy these five legal requirements:

1. A clear **offer** to perform specific works for a price

2. **Unconditional acceptance** of that offer

3. **Consideration** – this means exchanging your goods, works or services for something of value

3. An **intention** to create a legally binding contract *now*

5. **Certain** (or definite) terms.

All the above five legal requirements are *essential* for your small works contract to be a legal contract.

In practice, these requirements are surprisingly easy to meet. Before you work for a new client, she will often ask you to send her a proposal or quote:

- Your quote is an *offer* to provide specific goods, works or services for a price

- Your quote can be *accepted* by email, telephone call, returning a reply slip or when your client pays your first invoice

- Your quote asks for *something of value* (often money) in return for goods, works or services. What lawyers call *consideration* is anything of value.

The first three legal requirements are easily ticked off. When it comes to intention, then for business-to-business (B2B) proposals, *the intention to create a contract* is presumed to exist. If your proposal is business-to-consumer (B2C), then there is no such presumption, so getting your contract signed is even more important.

Although not related to contract formation, for most B2C contracts English law adds a 14-day cooling-off period[6] which helps to ensure your client intends to contract, and is not being pressured or bullied into it.

The last requirement – *certain terms* – is the most difficult aspect for contract writers and it is where you should focus your attention.

Why Do You Need Certain Terms? Any contract – for even the smallest project – should set out what the parties have agreed with certainty.

Your small works contract should provide certainty for the *parties*. Your client needs to know how much she will have to pay for the works, and you need to know which goods, works or services you are required to provide.

Your small works contract should also give certainty for *outsiders*, so that an independent third party (e.g. a judge) can immediately understand everything that both parties have agreed to do. If your small works contract only makes sense because of information you personally have inside your head, then a court may not be able to interpret it or enforce it.

Small works contracts need certain, not vague, terms to create a legally binding agreement.

4

SIMPLE CONTRACTS CREATE CONFIDENCE

The aim of your contract should be to record your agreement, safeguard your business and avoid disputes – all without annoying your client.

Legal documents have a bad reputation … they are not designed to be used to manage the project or relationships between the parties, but are legal sticks to beat the other side with when the project fails. They have become tools for pointing the finger of blame – rather than tools to help your client get specialist expertise, or tools to help you do business.

Even if you have been in business for many years, your client may never have done this sort of project before. Just because you have always done it your way, doesn't mean your client wants to do it that way. A small works contract needs to clarify your client's roles and responsibilities and give her confidence in you as her contractor.

In a series of recent interviews, clients told me there was a lack of clarity on the thorny issue of money, low confidence in their contractors and an underlying feeling of unhappiness.

Clients did not trust that:

■ Their builder understood what they really wanted to achieve (but never asked about)

- They knew what facilities, instructions, approval, directions and instalments they were responsible for (and how long they would have to pay any invoices)

- Their builder would communicate with as much information or as frequently as they needed to maintain their confidence in them and the project

- Their builder would do their best to resolve any issues when they were unhappy with the works, progress or the finished project.

For a consumer contract, English law requires you to provide various items of information before your client sign (or e-sign) on the dotted line and this is the bare minimum: main characteristics of your works, your contact details[7], the price she will have to pay (including taxes), when you will perform the works, your complaints handling policy, and how long your small works contract will last.

Be Clear About Your Dreams

A millionaire businessman dreamed of the construction of an Arts and Craft style house to be called Maison d'Or (House of Gold) in St Aubin, Jersey. It took 3 years to build at a cost of £4m and the client was so unhappy, he demolished it. The court recorded the absence of 'certain documents and procedures which are generally regarded as critical to a satisfactory outcome' like contracts and a specification.

One of the features of this case is the absence of any written record of what Mr McGlinn wanted at the outset and, in particular, what standard of finish he required at Maison d'Or ... a point he repeatedly made was that it had not been designed or built in accordance with the exceptionally high standards that he had asked for. This, inevitably, led to numerous disputes as to what precisely it was that he had required, given the absence of any written record or clear design brief.[8]

5

SIMPLE CONTRACTS SAFEGUARD YOUR BUSINESS

A precise record is one of the best ways of limiting your liability as it clearly sets out the tasks that each of you is responsible for. A clear scope of works is also the best way of explaining what you are not involved with; e.g. obtaining planning, connecting to existing utilities, designing the works, and so on.

You are probably great at describing the goods, works and services (I will refer to these collectively as 'works') you will provide and the price your client will pay. Although these items are critical, your small works contract should also:

■ **Define a clear scope of works:** Accuracy is essential to manage your client's expectations of what is/is not included in your price and to ensure that you can recover the cost of any changes to those works. The scope of works should be written so that your client can read and understand it, so minimise the industry jargon.

> **TIP:** Check that your client can tell when the works are complete.
> [Chapter 9]

■ **Explain how the works can be changed:** Under English law, a small works contract – and the works under that contract – cannot be varied except by creating a new contract. As this is impractical, your small works contract should include a simple procedure allowing changes to the works, or the contract. Your client hates surprises at the end, so it is best to agree extra costs or time *before* you implement the changes. If your change process is too complex or impractical, it may be ignored or circumvented.[9]

> **TIP:** Check that your change process will avoid surprising your client at the end – that she will understand how much extra she will pay for any changes to the works and how much longer they will take before they happen. [Chapter 14]

■ **Define responsibility for areas outside your expertise:** Your small works contract should precisely describe the limits of your responsibility, by clarifying what you are not responsible for. Otherwise your client may (mistakenly) assume you are doing everything she needs. This clarity helps to manage your client's expectations.

> **TIP:** Check that your small works contract sets out what you are not doing. [Chapter 9]

■ **Contain an escape clause:** If you discover that your client cannot and will not pay for the works you have provided (which you cannot take back as they are now fixed to her land and owned by her), or if your client discovers that you are not competent, or it becomes apparent that your client's project is no longer achievable, it may be sensible to swiftly end your contractual relationship. Your small works contract is not intended to be an agreement to work together indefinitely!

> **TIP:** Check that your small works contract for consumers includes a cancellation period [Chapter 18] as well as a mutual right to terminate. [Chapter 19]

26

6

SIMPLE CONTRACTS AVOID DISPUTES

Construction disputes are frequently caused by[10] the parties failing to:

- Understand/comply with the contract's obligations

- Create an accurate error-free contract

- Use the procedures in the contract.

If you create a small works contract that is easy to read, easy to understand and easy to use then you will avoid those key causes of disputes.

Easy to Read: Your small works contract will be easy to read if it has clear headings, short sentences and simple words. It is a myth that contracts need dense text, multiple cross-references or a complex structure.

A 500-word small works contract helps you avoid disputes because:

- *Your client will read it:* the short length of your contract will encourage your client to read it from start to finish.

- *Your client can negotiate it:* an easy-to-read small works contract acts as a checklist for negotiation.

- *Your client can check that it records what you agreed:* simple words mean your client can immediately verify whether the document is an accurate reflection of your agreement.

If your client does not read your small works contract, then she definitely won't understand it.

Easy to Understand: Your small works contract will be easy to understand if it avoids the jargon and technical terms prevalent in your sector. It is a myth that only lawyers should be able to understand the impact and intent of your contract.

A 500-word small works contract helps you avoid disputes because:

- *Your client will have the confidence to raise queries:* with clear and crisp content, your client knows what each word and each paragraph means, and will not be afraid to check if something does not make sense.

- *Your client will take responsibility:* when your small works contract is easy to understand, then the parties can resolve legal and practical issues quickly, without the need to get lawyers involved.

If your client does not understand your small works contract, then she definitely won't use it.

Easy to Use: Your small works contract will be easy to use if the parties can find the information they need because it is designed with them in mind. It is a myth that contracts should cover everything the parties can possibly think of, resulting in tedious length. Once your small works contract is long enough to create certainty [Parts B and C], stop.

A 500-word small works contract helps you avoid disputes because:

- *Your small works contract builds trust:* when both parties can use your contract they are more likely to find ways to make it really work, in the process becoming more collaborative.

- *Your client wants to comply:* a clear contract leaves no scope for debate about what she is meant to do – there is less chance that she will ignore important duties like providing instructions, access, approval and managing changes.

PART

B

HOW YOU CAN WRITE THE BARE MINIMUM

Before you start, you need a simple process to help you avoid relying on incomplete proposals, estimates or quotes. [Chapter 7]

This is the bare minimum you need and your client expects:

- **WHO? PARTIES:** your contract should explain who is paying for the works (the client) and who is carrying them out (the contractor). [Chapter 8]

- **WHAT? WORKS:** your contract should specify precisely the works *required* for the project, and what is not included in your price. [Chapter 9]

Each chapter looks at some of the common errors, the risks of not writing each element simply and what happens if your small works contract includes nothing on that topic.

7

BEFORE YOU START WRITING YOUR SMALL WORKS CONTRACT

There are a number of stages to writing any document, and these apply to works contracts from a single page (like a 500-word contract) to 200 pages.

- **Readers:** Your small works contract will be read by the parties, legal and business advisers, and, if you're unlucky, an adjudicator or a judge. You should write it to be read by all those people.

- **Users:** You and your client actually have to use your small works contract, so make it user-friendly.

- **Your Purpose:** There are a number of different purposes for your small works contract (see below) and you need to decide – before you start writing – which you are going to focus on.

- **Content:** This book sets out the content that your small works contract needs: the bare minimum, plus client-centred content and extra clauses to make it really effective. You should only start writing when you know what you need.

- **Order:** Despite myths to the contrary, there is no fixed structure or order for the contents of your small works contract (or any contract). To make sure it gets read first, you should explain how your works meet your client's expectations. You can group each party's obligations into separate sections or columns to make them easy to find, or list them chronologically.

- **Write:** How you write your small works contract is a matter of preference – typed, dictated or hand-written all have the same end result. You can even create it in graphic form. The key is to start from a blank piece of paper and use this book to write down just what you think your small works contract really needs, and then stop. *Try not to recycle a previously-used document!*

- **Edit:** This is how you check it contains the contents you think are essential, as well as ensuring your small works contract is accurate, brief and clear.

What Is Your Purpose?

Many contract writers never stop and think *why* they are writing and using them. A specific purpose will focus your writing making it clearer and crisper.

Do you want your small works contract to:

- *safeguard only your interests* ('cover your back')? A one-sided document is likely to be unfair, cause friction or confuse your client. It is better to create a small works contract which balances and safeguards both your interests.

- *be watertight or bombproof?* Sadly, there is no such thing.

- *act as a form of insurance* in the event of a complaint or dispute? If so, you are missing the opportunity to guide your client on how to behave while you are working together. It should not merely explain how to 'clean up' after you've made a mess of the project.

The true purpose of a small works contract is to *clarify* your scope of works (that you will be performing), the price (that your client will be paying), your/your client's aims, and explain how risks will be managed.

8

THE PARTIES INVOLVED

Recording the identity of the parties accurately in your small works contract is the easiest part of writing your contract. It really doesn't matter who they are. In English law you are free to contract with just about *anyone*.[11]

In your small works contract, the named contractor is the company that has to do the work. The named client is the person or company who has to pay. It is almost impossible to persuade the court that you made a mistake. In addition to the legal aspect, the identity of your client is a matter of practicality. As tempting as the white beaches may seem, a company with its registered office in the Turks and Caicos Islands is hard to contact and even harder to sue.

Avoiding Common Errors

To ensure your small works contract names the parties correctly, you should:

- Use the correct company name, especially if it is part of a large group of similarly-named companies

- Insert the company number and registered office for a limited company, the trading address for partnerships, the full names and addresses of individuals, and any separate address for notices (including emails, if relevant)

- Check which clients are signing – especially if the property has many people living there

- Check which people are authorised to sign the small works contract

- Using these details, either print or email a copy of your small works contract and ask your client to sign or reply to confirm their agreement. You can also use electronic signing tools like DocuSign or Adobe Sign.

When you are providing a proposal or quote, this is the time to be clear about which company will be carrying out the works and to ask which company or individuals will be paying for them. It is not enough to hope that the person you met owns the land on which you will do the works or that she will be the one writing the cheques.

Does It Really Matter?

Keeping an Eye on the Details

A scaffolding company provided a quote to MCR Property Group (MCR) for certain works, and MCR responded with their purchase order on the letterhead of Palmloch Limited. The purchase order asked the scaffolding company to invoice Palmloch Limited.

In a dispute over payment, the scaffolding company started an adjudication [see Glossary] against MCR who argued that they were not a party to the contract (formed from the quote and purchase order). MCR was just a trading name and didn't legally exist.

The adjudicator made an award asking MCR to pay and a judge agreed that although Palmloch were the correct contract party, there was no lack of clarity or ambiguity in bringing the claim against MCR.[12] The judge said *a reasonable recipient … would have understood the use of the trading name as an unambiguous reference to Palmloch.*

Even though this decision helped the contractor, the proceedings were costly and time-consuming.

Do You Need to Include the Parties? Yes. If your small works contract does not correctly identify the parties responsible for carrying out its obligations, then your contract lacks certainty and it is not legally binding. Getting the parties right is *critical*.

Why Should You Keep It Simple? There are four reasons you should keep it simple. Firstly, it is incredibly quick and free to clarify the correct details for the parties (e.g. using a Companies House search[13]); secondly, getting it right means you know precisely which corporate entity or individuals you are contracting with; thirdly, the consequences of getting it wrong are significant.

The fourth reason to be clear about the parties to the small works contract is technical (in the legal sense). In English law, a principle called 'privity of contract' means only those parties listed on the small works contract can bring claims against each other for breach of contract.[14] The client cannot be sued by a subcontractor or supplier if you fail to pay them – even if they knew it was your client's money funding the project. Similarly, your client can only sue your subcontractors or suppliers under the contract if your contract allows her to. Knowing with whom you are entering into a small works contract is relatively simple, legally critical and practically essential.

How You Can Write It Simply: Your small works contract should correctly record three things:

1. the parties

2. their addresses for notices

3. one of:

   - the company name, registered number and registered office *for corporations (including limited liability partnerships or LLPs)*

   - the partnership name, the name of all current partners and the principal office *for partnerships*[15]

   - the trading name, the owner and the principal office *for a sole trader*

- the full names and addresses for any individuals.

Including the parties' details at the front of your small works contract is part of gathering all the key information in one place (see sample small works contracts at www.just500words.co.uk).

As well as naming the parties, your small works contract should be signed on behalf of each party by a properly authorised person. In England/Wales that means:

- a director or company secretary *for companies or corporations*

- all or a specific number of partners (as set out in their partnership agreement) *for partnerships*

- the individuals *for consumer clients* or the business owner *for a sole trader.*

Partners, directors and company representatives sign as agents and your contract is treated as being made by the company or partnership. This method of signing creates a simple contract [see Glossary] and the parties can bring claims for its breach for 6 years from completion of the works.

Signing your small works contract is best practice as it shows both parties have agreed to everything in it. In practice, your small works contract can be accepted by email, text, phone call or by any relevant act such as starting the works, or paying the first instalment.

9

THE WORKS BEING PROVIDED

Your small works contract is the tool that will enable your client to get specialist goods, works or services to meet a particular need. Your client will want to know what works you are providing, that you are competent to provide them, and that those works will help her to achieve specific aims or meet her expectations. [Part C]

Are you:

- Installing specialist equipment which your client is buying?

- Choosing goods or materials to meet a specific purpose or output requirement?

- Carrying out demolition works, constructing a new building or extending her home?

- Providing expertise to coordinate and supervise subcontractors?

- Designing a project to meet your client's requirements? or

- All of the above?

Scope is critical for all contracts – the IACCM puts the lack of clear scope first in their Top 10 pitfalls to avoid in contracting.[16] It is considered critical by contract writers (although less so by those who negotiate contracts).

Avoiding Common Errors

To ensure your small works contract identifies the works precisely you should:

- Confirm any goods that you need to order

- Describe the works accurately so your client can tell when they are complete

- Explain what elements you are not responsible for

- List, if you can, distinct tasks and services that you will perform

- Split the works into chunks (sections) that your client can visualise

- Refer to your quote for the scope of works, drawings and other works documents that clarify the project.

Your description of the works should ensure that your client clearly understands what you are providing and what you are not providing. Remember, from your client's perspective she is more interested in the outputs or deliverables – what will it look like, how big will it be, and how will it perform? Focus on the benefits and results for your client; not how many bricks, people or weeks are required.

Does It Really Matter?

It's Not Enough to Be Vague

In a claim relating to a $60m luxury Caribbean resort, the court was surprised to find that the documents were sparse and the witnesses erratic and unreliable – the project unravelled spectacularly. The court found that:

Harlequin [the client] paid ICE, its contractor, around $52 million. They did so, not only without any sort of written contract, but without any detailed agreement as to the scope of the works to be

> *carried out, the monitoring of those works, or their valuation …*
> *McGovern J described this situation as 'extraordinary'. That is, if*
> *anything, an under-statement. In my view, for a project of this size,*
> *the fact that there were no financial controls whatsoever beggars all*
> *belief.*
>
> It's not just small works which suffer from poor paperwork and
> vague scope!

Do You Need To Include the Works? Yes. If your small works contract does not identify the works, your document is too uncertain to be a contract.

Why Should You Keep It Simple? Your small works contract should record an agreement to pay for/provide specific works, at a defined price, to be completed by a particular date. Without a clear scope of works, how can your client possibly:

- be sure that she is paying a fair price for the works?

- evaluate if you are making sufficient progress against the schedule?

- determine what is a change to the works?

- pin-point when you have provided everything you promised?

How You Can Write It Simply: On most projects, you are providing a combination of goods, plant and equipment, works, information and documents, as well as services such as supervision, design or project management. You are the best person to describe precisely what you will do for your client. Your description needs to be really clear – from the client's perspective – so avoid jargon and technical terms.

Your small works contract can describe the goods, works and services you will provide accurately, briefly and clearly:

We will carry out the Works <outline> described in <insert quote, specification, drawings with date/ref for each>.

Your small works contract will be accurate if the description of the works makes sense to the parties and other people. It needs to have enough detail and information to allow an outsider to decide whether you have done what your client asked for. You need to make sure the reference number, version, date, author and all identifying details of any relevant documents are recorded as these may be superseded during the contract negotiations and construction.

Your contract will be more accurate if it also says clearly what you are *not* going to do. This is a simple means of excluding your responsibility for works outside your expertise, which others are undertaking (e.g. design), or to clarify possible areas of overlap. Your small works contract can say:

> We will neither provide nor be responsible for <insert tasks, services or elements of the project which are not part of the Works>.

Your small works contract will be brief and clear if it contains all the necessary information without ambiguities or inconsistencies. The description in your small works contract should match and reflect the details in the works documents (e.g. quote, specification and drawings). Your description of the works is never going to be 100% comprehensive, but writing it simply ensures your client can read your outline and understand your role.

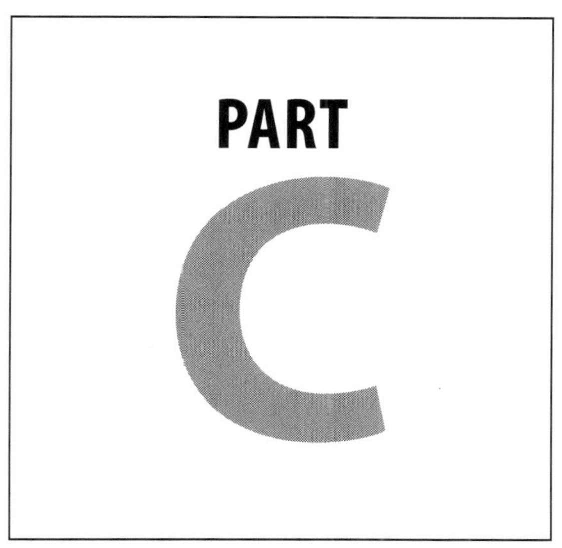

HOW YOU CAN WRITE CLIENT-CENTRED CONTENT

Without parties and works [Part B], there is *never* a contract. But realistically a building contract, even for a small works project, needs the parties' agreement as to the time and cost.[17]

And once you start talking time and cost, you really need to reflect the client's aims and expectations on quality as well as any project-specific aims.

The four client-centred contents are:

- **WHEN? TIME:** your contract should include a date when you will start the works and a date when your client can expect they will be completed. [Chapter 10]

- **HOW MUCH? COST:** your contract should explain how much your client will have to pay for the works and when. [Chapter 11]

- **WHAT OUTPUTS? QUALITY:** your contract should define your client's preferred quality standards for the goods, works and services. [Chapter 12]

- **WHAT EXPECTATIONS? AIMS:** your contract should set out any other aims or expectations for the works. [Chapter 13]

This Part will help you understand what to write in your small works contract and why you should keep it simple. Each chapter looks at some of the risks of not writing each element simply and what happens if your small works contract includes nothing on that topic.

You can easily write the critical content that you need to create a legally binding agreement, dramatically improving the clarity of your small works contract.

10

THE TIME TO ACT

One-third of UK construction projects finish late[18], even once the contractual completion date has been extended to take account of changes and events after the works were started. For most clients, time is less important than cost or quality. However you need to ask what your client's key objective is: time, cost, quality or something else, as it hugely influences decisions on how changes are managed during the project. [Chapter 14]

For most B2C small works, your client may be keen to know when you are going to start the works, but rarely needs you to *guarantee* that you will complete those works by a specific date. Business clients tend to take a different view, as the success of a project can depend on meeting completion dates agreed with their bank, purchaser, tenants or any occupiers.

Avoiding Common Errors

A serious mistake in small works contracts is to copy legal jargon and refer to 'time of the essence'. This means if you are late your client can cancel or terminate the contract, and she may refuse to pay for works already completed.[19] If your contract includes a procedure to extend the time for completion, or for delay damages then 'time of the essence' makes no sense – your client has contradictory remedies for late completion. She needs one or the other.

Your small works contract needs to keep the works to the schedule your client is expecting. Your contract should:

- include a *start date* for the works – this is when you will be allowed onto the site or into your client's home (and not before),

- specify the proposed *completion date* for the works, and

- provide a change management process to move that *completion date*.

Your contract can also, but need not, include your promise to progress the works and attend the site regularly (ideally specifying your proposed working hours). For B2B contracts, it can include a remedy if you are late in completing the works – in the form of delay damages [Glossary].

Does It Really Matter?

How Slow Can You Go?

In a series of contracts for works related to a nursing home and associated accommodation the client became increasingly frustrated with progress. The client wrote letters to the contractor requiring it to complete the works *as soon as possible* and *as a matter of urgency* before sending a letter terminating the contract for these delays.

The court had to consider the respective rights and remedies of the parties relating to time. Its first problem was that *there was virtually no reliable documentation which provided evidence of what had been agreed, and between whom*. It was not even clear when the works started ... and any completion dates originally agreed had since been waived.

The frustration of the client and her decision to end the contract was partly driven by lack of clarity over the time for completing

---

> the works, how her initial expectations as to completion could change and whether there was any obligation on the contractor to make sensible progress.[20]

Do You Need to Include Time? You don't have to include a *start date* to create a contract, however your client will want more than a 'this year/next year/sometime' indication of when her project will start. You should aim to give your client as much notice as possible of when you can start as this helps manage her expectations.

You don't have to include a *completion date* to create a contract. If you don't include a specific completion date or an agreed works period, legislation implies a contractual term that you will complete the works within a 'reasonable time'. What counts as a reasonable time depends *on the circumstances which actually exist*[21] and means you will not progress negligently or unreasonably. This vague requirement could allow you to be slow but steady – which may not be what your client wants.

You don't have to include a specific *rate of progress* in your contract. However, if you don't there is no implied obligation on you to attend site regularly or work diligently.[22]

You don't have to include a *right for your client to deduct delay damages* if you are late in completing the works. But, if you don't, your client can sue you for breach of that obligation, resulting in a larger award of damages, as well as suffering the time and cost of resolving the dispute.

Why Should You Keep It Simple? Having a realistic schedule for starting, progressing and finishing the works will provide a standard against which your client can measure your progress and performance. Having a simple remedy if you're late can avoid complex disputes over time issues.

How You Can Write It Simply: Your small works contract should not over-promise on the schedule. Any completion date, even if it includes some leeway or contingency, will help both parties focus on making progress:

> We will start the Works on <insert start date>, make regular and reasonable progress, and complete the Works by <insert completion date>.

Although I have rarely seen delay damages in a small works contract (almost never in a consumer contract), this remedy provides a simple means of recovering some of the costs or losses associated with slow progress. It can also build trust with your client to offer to allow her to deduct (even nominal) damages for each week that you are late in completing the works:

> If the Works are not complete by the extended completion date you can deduct £<insert figures> for every week of delay.

If your small works contract includes delay damages, it must also include an extension procedure [Chapter 14]. The parties have to be able to extend the completion date for specific events that might delay your progress; e.g. if your client fails to give access or orders changes to the works. The courts will not allow your client to act in a way which causes you delay, and then also recover damages for that delayed period – when it is her fault.

11

THE PRICE YOUR CLIENT WILL PAY

The problem with talking money is that everyone *thinks* they are hard done to.

The problem with *not* talking money is that everyone *will definitely* be hard done to!

Many construction disputes, especially adjudications, revolve around whether the contractor has been paid what it believes is a 'fair' or reasonable price for the works provided. Cash is king, or as the judge Lord Denning famously once said *the very lifeblood of the enterprise*[23]. Knowing *how much* will be paid and *when* is crucial to both parties.

Most[24] UK construction projects are carried out for a fixed price or lump sum. This means that your quote gives a total price[25] for a specific scope of works and, once that quote is agreed, your client agrees to pay that price, irrespective of what it actually costs you to carry out those works. You bear the risk that your price is too low and your client bears the risk that your price is too high.

According to an IACCM Survey[26], price is the third most negotiated term and, together with price changes, the most frequently cited cause for disputes.

Avoiding Common Errors

Your small works contract should:

- confirm that the price is a fixed price for the stated scope,

- state how much your client will pay (for a consumer client, your price must include value added tax),

- set out how your price will be invoiced in instalments using a payment schedule; e.g. based on percentages of the works, regular equal instalments, or fixed sums on completion of specific elements or parts of the works, and

- (optionally) include rates to make it easier to price any extra works.

If your small works contract lacks clarity on *works*, *price* and *time*, you are effectively asking your client to sign up to open-ended liability to pay for an open-ended set of works to be completed when you choose.

For a construction contract (most B2B contracts), your small works contract must also meet the minimum requirements for a payment process set out in the Construction Acts 1996 and 2009.

Does It Really Matter?

'State of the Art' Yet Incomplete Paperwork

Mr Clarke asked ACT Construction to construct 'the job' (a state of the art coach station) for no more than £815,000. Negotiations proceeded rather informally, relying on honour rather than legal terms. The correspondence revealed that neither the works nor the price was *defined with any precision*. The question was whether there was enough certainty for it to be a contract.

The Court of Appeal said *Even if there is no 'formal' contract, there may still be an agreement to carry out work ... even if a price has not been agreed. Provided there is an instruction to do work and an*

> *acceptance of that instruction, there is a contract and the law will imply into it an obligation to pay a reasonable sum for that work.*[27]
>
> The court told Mr Clarke that his project had cost a cool £1.5m.

Do You Need To Include a Price? There are two aspects to consider: *what* you want your client to pay for the works and *when* you want her to pay.

If your small works contract does not contain a price, or a means of determining the price, it *may* be too uncertain for a contract. But once you get started, even if you have not yet agreed a price, legislation implies a contractual term that your client will pay a reasonable price for the works.[28]

For consumer clients, you are free to decide how and when you want your client to pay the price. For business clients, the Construction Acts entitle you to be paid in instalments[29] and implies contractual terms if you fail to include them.

Why Should You Keep It Simple? If you don't agree a price in your small works contract, then you client has no idea *what* to pay. A consumer client can challenge your price if it is not prominent and transparent. A business client may refuse to pay if the price is not clear.

If you agree a price but not the payment terms, your client doesn't know *how* or *when* to pay. Your contract needs a simple payment procedure. The more complex it is, the less likely your client will follow it. If your business client doesn't pay on time, you have an implied right to suspend any or all of your works, and charge interest on late payments [Chapter 17]. Relying on these remedies can destroy your relationship with your client irrevocably. It is far better to have simple procedures that anyone can follow.

How You Can Write It Simply: For consumer clients, the simplest way to write *what, how* and *when* your client has to pay is to set out a schedule of payments:

You will pay the Price £<insert> fairly against our correct invoices. We will send invoices stating the sum we consider payable and our calculation as follows: invoice <number> for £<insert> by <date>. [*repeat as necessary*].

For business clients, your small works contract needs this and extra detail including payment and pay-less notices [Glossary], as well as your right to suspend the services for non-payment:

Due dates are the invoice dates; final dates (when you need to pay) are <insert> days after the invoice dates.

You will send a pay-less notice showing the sum you will pay and your calculation at least <insert> days before the final date, if you intend to pay less than the invoiced amount.

If you neither send a pay-less notice nor pay in full, we can suspend carrying out any of the Works until paid in full, and you will extend the completion date.

Although this is not mandatory for consumer contracts, pay-less notices prevent unwelcome surprises and smooth the payment process to prevent disputes. Instead of referring to due and final dates – which is confusing terminology – consumer contracts can state that your client will pay your invoices 'within <agreed number> days' and any pay-less notice will be served '<insert> days before payment is due'.

12

THE QUALITY YOU WANT

The most costly construction disputes often relate to the quality of the finished project. Did it meet the client's explicit and implicit expectations and objectives? To take just a few examples:

- Should a brand new home, costing nearly £1m, have hundreds of snagging items?

- Should the Torre di Pisa have leant, even before it was completed?

- Should the Millennium Bridge have wobbled when pedestrians crossed the River Thames, London?

- Should the spires on the churches at Chesterfield, England or Verchin, France have twisted?

Achieving the expected quality is a core aim of any project.

Avoiding Common Errors

Your small works contracts could fall into the lazy option of not stating the quality standards required by your client. Your scope of work might be sufficient but its quality may not be in language your client can understand and agree to. Your small works contract should describe (or refer to documents which describe):

- the functional and aesthetic requirements of the works once completed,

- the precise specification of goods or materials,

- any tests or inspections that the works (or parts of them) need to pass, and

- the standard for the performance of any services including design, workmanship and supervision.

Your contract also needs to distinguish between two measures for quality: an *input* measure (the level of expertise you will use) and an *output* measure (the extent to which the finished works do what your client wants them to). Essentially, this is the difference between reasonable skill and care (input) and fitness for purpose (output).

Unless your small works contract says so, you are not guaranteeing that the works will achieve your client's specific desired results.

Does It Really Matter?

Don't Burn Your Popcorn

Whether your project meets the client's quality requirements can make a *huge* difference.

In 2003, ADT agreed to supply a fire suppression system for a proposed (not yet built) popcorn factory in Pontefract. ADT used a standard specification to describe what it was providing and what the system was meant to achieve. Essentially, both the client and the contractor focused their efforts on getting the factory operational to provide popcorn to cinemas for the Christmas buying bonanza. Neither of the parties gave a second thought as to the precise performance requirements of the system.

Although ADT was paid just £9,000, the client claimed £110m for its losses following a catastrophic fire in 2005. The client argued that ADT failed to provide a fire suppression system that was 'fit for its intended purpose' (a high standard). As the contract said

---

> nothing about what that purpose might be, the Court of Appeal said ADT only had to use reasonable skill and care (average competence) in designing and providing the system.
>
> The crux of the case was that the contract did not specify any particular purpose or any quality or performance standards – ADT and its client both argued (after the event) that a different standard should apply. The client recovered £34m.[30]

Do You Need to Include Quality Standards? No. If your small works contract is silent on the fitness of works, quality of goods and materials, or performance of services, it is still a contract. Contractual terms will be implied by legislation or cases so that:

- goods will be of satisfactory quality,

- goods will be reasonably fit for their intended purpose (provided your client has made their purpose known and it is reasonable for her to rely on your skills in selecting those goods), and

- works and services will be carried out with reasonable skill and care.

These standards are the bare minimum your client will expect from you. Reasonable skill and care simply means that you are averagely competent, based on current industry standards, and that you act in accordance with generally accepted industry practices.[31] This is a more poetic explanation:

The standard is that of the reasonable average. The law does not require of a professional man that he be a paragon, combining the qualities of polymath and prophet.[32]

Why Should You Keep It Simple? Your client is probably hoping for a little more than Average Contractors Ltd when she hands over her cash for the project. She doesn't really expect materials which are simply OK or services that are merely competent.

Clarity helps you to know with certainty what you are being asked to do and to avoid defects – which result from poorly defined or poorly met quality standards. Keeping it simple at the start pays dividends for the whole life of the completed project (which can be many decades).

As your client will have decided to use you based on her evaluation of your skills, standards of performance and experience (as set out online or in your proposal or quote), then she shouldn't have to rely on inadequate *implied* terms. If your client is a consumer, any promises you have made about your competency, performance standards and expertise form part of your contract.

How You Can Write It Simply: If your client wants works that meet a specific standard or are reasonably fit for a specific purpose, your small works contract needs to state that relevant standard or purpose. Your quote may refer to or contain a scope of works, drawings and other works documents which describe the applicable standards.

You should agree the exact standards you want with your client. Your contract must be precise.

Your small works contract can oblige you to meet these quality standards by stating:

> We will use reasonable skill and care to ensure the Works when completed meet the standards, or are fit for the purposes, described in <insert relevant document; e.g. the scope of works>.

For projects with a contract administrator [Glossary], you could give them the role of approving the quality of the works; e.g. 'We will complete the works to the reasonable satisfaction of <name>' (assuming they are experienced, knowledgeable and impartial). It is not appropriate for your client to act as contract administrator as she is not sufficiently objective.

13

THE AIMS YOU NEED
TO ACHIEVE

There are three types of aims that your small works contract needs to take account of:

Core Aims: These aims are the standard trinity of *time*, *cost* and *quality*. Your small works contract has to strike a balance between getting the works completed on time, at a price that fairly reflects the scope and risks, and carried out to the desired quality. These aspects were covered in Chapters 10, 11 and 12 respectively.

Client Specific: While every project contains certain run-of-the-mill aspects, each client has her own needs and aims (her *why*) and each project and site has its own unique challenges. Some of the client-specific aims may also be influenced by your marketing materials and pre-contract information. Under the Consumer Rights Act 2015, a consumer client is entitled to rely on the pre-contract information that you provide to her as being a binding term of your small works contract.

Trust: Although each party has its own individual *why*, the parties involved in a project have to work together. You will need to share information and documents, be honest with each other as to the resources you have or your client needs, provide accurate data and instructions on time, and not prevent others from getting on with their tasks. Trust is essential to construction, as it is an inherently collaborative process, with everyone working to a common goal.

Avoiding Common Errors

Your small works contract should not:

- Ignore the problem that your client seeks a solution to. Don't assume your client even knows what success would look like for her. Every problem has a number of alternative solutions, and finding the best solution requires you to ask great questions. [Chapter 20]

- Overlook the importance of trust. Your small works contract should not treat your client as an adversary, or attempt to ensure you retain the legal and moral high ground. You need to set out how you and your client will work together.

Does It Really Matter?

Working Together

A contractor's proposal said that it would provide its clients with *a detailed easy-to-understand timetable describing the renovation activity – a complete 'what will be happening and when' timeline that you can monitor daily, if you so desire, for total peace of mind ... this is not a promise; it is a guarantee – a contractual guarantee ...* [33] The contractor promised it would cure the clients of their 'nest stress'; i.e. stress from a home which did not meet their needs.

The works did not proceed according to plan. After months of missed completion dates the family moved back into their house and found power failures, faults, leaks, incomplete works, defective heating and so on. *You never knew when something would go wrong or what problem would be discovered next, and some of the workmen were still coming and going.*

> The clients, at the end of their tether, terminated the contract and the court held that such action was well within their rights given the contractor's history of poor performance.

CLIENT-SPECIFIC AIMS

Do You Need Aims? If you don't state what your client wants to achieve then your small works contract will be certain enough to be a contract, but you will never know if the project and your role in it was a success. If you don't state which is the most important aim then it will be much harder to make informed decisions about potential changes to the project.

Why Should You Keep It Simple? Your client doesn't really care about your reviews, trade body memberships, or how big your office is. She wants to know that you can solve her problem. If your small works contract makes no reference to her aims, how can she check that you have properly understood her needs? A simple statement of her challenge or the aims of her project will manage her expectations and set the foundations for success.

How You Can Write It Simply: As each client is different, you need to reflect back what your client explained when you asked her why she was doing this project and the problems she needs you to solve:

> Your expectations for the Works are <insert> and your priority is <pick one of time, cost, or quality; or insert other>. If we have misunderstood, please tell us immediately.

TRUST AIMS

Do You Need To Trust Your Client? In law, no. In practice, yes.

Many small works contracts are designed for the small percentage of clients who are difficult to deal with: pay late, never provide instructions, complain bitterly over the slightest slip, and make your working life unpleasant. Surely it is better to have good expectations of all your clients, while being realistic enough to know that sometimes you will be disappointed.

If you are working on a construction project, there is an implied obligation that the parties will co-operate with each other. You cannot help your client if she does not give you access, information about her needs, instructions and approvals. Your client cannot achieve her aims and expectations if you don't keep communicating with each other.

Why Should You Keep It Simple? Although you may both understand in principle that trust is essential, sometimes you and your client (and even the project team) can forget that you are doing this project *together*. Collaboration, trust, and integrity do not come naturally to everyone.

Your small works contract can simply set out the behaviours you expect from your client and your client expects from you, to build your credibility and demonstrate your competence.

How You Can Write It Simply: Even clients and contractors with considerable experience can be surprised when they find out they are *obliged* to work together to complete a project. Your contract can spell out your understanding of your client's role and the conduct you expect from her. You can set your project on the right course by simply stating:

The parties will collaborate on your project <describe>.

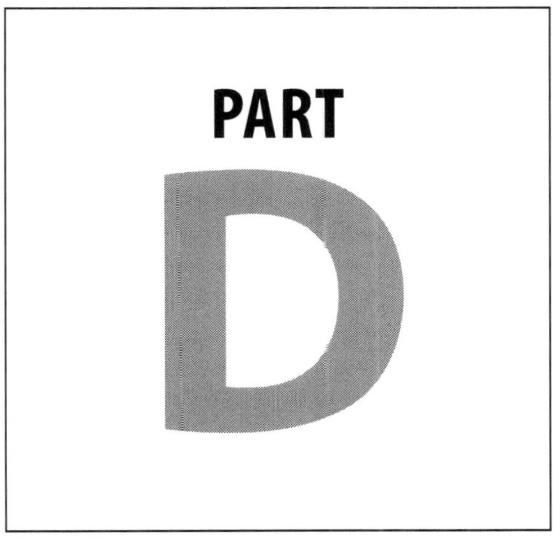

HOW YOU CAN WRITE EFFECTIVE SMALL WORKS CONTRACTS

Once your small works contract meets the five legal requirements [Part A], contains the bare minimum [Part B] and the client-centred content [Part C], it will be a legally binding agreement. As a result it creates obligations on both you and your client. If either party does not meet those obligations, the other can bring a claim for breach of the small works contract.

However, to be truly effective your small works contract requires a little more depth. It should:

- be 'workable' by including procedures on payment, managing changes to the works and extending the time to complete [Chapter 14],

- minimise the risks associated with small works [Chapter 15],

- prevent those and other risks undermining your business by limiting your liability [Chapter 16],

- set out some useful extra remedies in the event things do not go according to plan [Chapter 17] to help you avoid formal disputes, and

- allow your client to cancel the contract [Chapter 18] or both parties to terminate future works when necessary [Chapter 19].

14

PROCEDURES HELP YOUR PROJECT RUN SMOOTHLY

Contracts are not just about what works you are providing, but explain how you are going to work *with* your client. Your small works contract should set out the process of getting from where your client is now to where she wants to be. That path may be obvious to you as an experienced contractor, but it may not be clear to your client.

Procedures deal with everything from payment, communicating information, project modelling, assisting each other and managing changes, to remedies when the project goes wrong including how you resolve disputes. Procedures put some detail into the general principle of trust and co-operation. [Chapter 13]

Most contracts implicitly rely on industry practices, professional processes and standard behaviours to supplement their express terms. The vast majority of procedures are not written out in full. Some may exist in internal handbooks, some are 'too obvious' to reduce to writing and others are unwritten rules of conduct.

Avoiding Common Errors

Your small works contract should strike a balance between including too many procedures (bamboozling your client and making it inflexible) and too few (making it useless as a guide). A sensible compromise is to include the procedures essential to help you and your client work together:

- **Payment:** required to build trust, avoid disputes and (for business clients) meet the requirements of the Construction Acts 1996 and 2009. [Chapter 11]

- **Scope change:** setting out how/whether the works can be extended or varied, including how the parties will agree the impact of that change on the price being paid and the time to complete the works.

- **Time change:** allowing the completion date for the works to be extended if the parties agree changes or for other unexpected events. This is critical if your client has a right to delay damages. [Chapter 10]

- **Defects:** giving you the right to repair any minor defects during a fixed period. [Chapter 17]

- **Ending the contract:** a B2C contract requires a cooling-off period [Chapter 18] and you can include rights to cancel or terminate future works as well. [Chapter 19]

Most of these procedures are dealt with elsewhere so this chapter focuses on a change procedure.

Does It Really Matter?

Pragmatic and Practical Change Procedure

A change procedure, or variation clause, helps both you and your client. It allows your client to change the works to meet her and the project's changing requirements. It allows you to carry out the new works without having to re-tender.

The courts have reinforced the sensible use of a variations clause as its purpose is *to enable the [client] to alter the scope of the works*

> *to meet its requirements. As a project proceeds it may become clear that some change of mind is needed to attain the result now desired. That might be a simple realisation that something is no longer needed … or it might be for some other reasons such as lack of money, or a change in the requirements of the actual or prospective occupier or user.*[34]

Do You Need to Include a Change Procedure? No. However, if your small works contract does not expressly allow changes to the works, you would need to issue a new small works contract to create a new legally binding agreement for any additional works.

Once you allow changes to the works, you also need a procedure to change the completion date and/or schedule one if you want to be able to deduct delay damages [Chapter 10]. The courts will not allow your client to request changes, delay access or otherwise prevent you from completing the works by the completion date, *and* retain her right to recover damages for delay that *she* caused.

Why Should You Keep It Simple? Whilst it is inevitable that your client may *want* to change her mind, she may not understand the consequences of her instructions. Your change procedure needs to be simple and easy to follow. If not, it won't be used and the new works may be instructed verbally, leaving both of you wondering if you have a legally binding agreement for them.

Changes may also affect the time the works take (unless it is a like-for-like substitution; e.g. of different paint colours or door finishes) or the price you want to get paid. These should be agreed with your client before you carry out her instructions – it avoids surprises at the end of the project which tend to leave a long-lasting and nasty taste in her mouth. Your client is entitled to the information she needs from you to choose between the original plan and the revised proposals.

A simple extension procedure will allow you to extend the completion date so you both know what date you are aiming for, and limit your liability for damages from delays.

How You Can Write It Simply: To protect your client's budget and to prevent your client's requests overwhelming the original scope of works, you could include a limit on the costs or extra time required for those changes. The procedure can be as simple as:

> You can ask us to increase, decrease or modify the Works, or other aspects of this contract [provided your requests do not increase the Price/period for the Works by more than <insert figures>%]. Before we implement your request, we will both agree any changes to the Price and completion date.

Although many standard form construction contracts include long lists of events which can entitle you to more time, they generally fall into three basic categories: changes, client acts/omissions or uncontrollable events. Referring to these should be sufficient for your small works contract:

> You will extend the completion date for any changes to the Works, your own acts and omissions which delay completion, or events beyond the reasonable control of either party.

15

MANAGING RISK EVENTS

There is no such thing as a risk-free construction project.

Each site, each end-user, each design and each project team is unique. No-one can guarantee what will happen over the course of the next few months. There might be a global pandemic, steel prices might rise 200% overnight or a flash flood might wash away your site. Every construction project involves taking a calculated risk.

Your small works contract should help the parties manage those risks ('risks' are more accurately referred to as 'risk events').

Risk management is a 4-stage process:

1. Identify risk events: both common risks for small works projects and those specific to this project, this site, this part of the economic cycle, this client.

2. Analyse those risk events: you need to use your experience to estimate how likely each risk event is to occur and the consequences (for you, your client and the project) if they do. Your projects should not start until you and your client have identified and analysed relevant risk events.

3. Respond to those risk events: if there are too many risks or the analysis shows the project is not commercially viable, the best course of action might be to walk away. However, risk response

can take the form of insurance, acceptance (stuff happens), sharing (the consequences), mitigation (trying to avoid it) or management (e.g. change procedures).

4. Review those risks: as the project continues the risk profile will change and this is where collaborating and communicating regularly with your client is critical.

Avoiding Common Errors

A comprehensive contract would:

- state the specific risks that are allocated to an insurer (e.g. fire, flood, design liability) or one of the parties (e.g. supplier strikes) – in practice, many clients will presume that you have an adequate level of cover for the works being undertaken and you can reassure them about this in your proposal or estimate,

- include regular review procedures (e.g. changing the key objectives to reflect risks or events which have happened), and

- demonstrate how the consequences of specific risks are retained by, shared with or transferred between the parties.

Does It Really Matter?

Prudence for Pioneers

A few years after a new type of television mast was finished, it collapsed into a heap of mangled steel and was no longer transmitting signals. [This case took over a decade to get a conclusion in the courts!]

The House of Lords said *The project may be alluring. But the risks of injury to those engaged in it, or to others, or to both, may be so manifest and substantial and their elimination may be so difficult to ensure with reasonable certainty that the only proper course is to abandon the project altogether.*

> Although the contractor had argued that it could not walk away from the project because that was unthinkable, the judges disagreed and said that *the law requires even pioneers to be prudent.*[35]

Do You Need to Include Risks? No. However for a fixed price contract [Glossary], where the risks are not expressly stated then your client is entitled to assume that the time and cost consequences of any risk event that does occur is included in your price. If this is not how you have priced for the works then it is important your client understands the events which could change the completion date and those which will increase your price. Price issues are a major cause of client dissatisfaction.

If there are other unexpected or unforeseen events (like a global pandemic causing labour and supply chain issues, health and safety concerns, lockdowns on site activity, advice from various bodies on suspending works or keeping going) then these are best dealt with by communicating clearly with your client and agreeing how to proceed. Contracts should not be used to deal with every last possibility, but to provide a collaborative framework in which trust forms the basis for making decisions when the contract does not dictate a precise path.

Why Should You Keep It Simple? You could follow the style of most standard form contracts and include a long list of risk events that are more or less likely to occur – these cover a wide variety of events caused by the parties or third parties. Lists like these are often reviewed with a fine-tooth comb, amended and when something happens pored over to see if they cover the precise event that has occurred. However, essentially the thrust of these clauses is that you will want a chance to extend the completion date and/or review your prices for events beyond your control and which are not caused by your fault.

How You Can Write It Simply: Changes, client acts/omissions and uncontrollable events allow you more time under our extension procedure. Other events are changes to 'other aspects of this contract' and are covered by the change procedure. This should be sufficient for most small works contracts.

16

LIMITING YOUR LIABILITY

There are two main ways of limiting your liability for claims arising from your client's project in your small works contract. First, you can define and clarify the extent of your obligations and the works, so your client really understands what you are responsible for. Secondly, you can add limits on time and/or money on your liability for breach of contract, to reduce your exposure in the event you are at fault and face a disgruntled client.

Outside your contract, the best way of limiting your liability is to keep your promises.

Setting a maximum liability to any client on a project will help you reduce the risks to your business, may reduce your insurance premiums, and can be factored into your price. Your price should take into account the scope of your works [Chapter 9], and your analysis of the potential impact if risk events occur, including failing to meet your client's aims. [Part C]

Avoiding Common Errors

The most common error is not recognising that a clear scope of works is the best means of defining your liability and excluding other liability. You can state what you are and are not doing to avoid your client harbouring any doubts.

Another failure in small works contracts is to include limits on *your liability* which are neither simple nor clear, such as:

- a clause excluding liability for indirect or consequential losses, which are either not defined or defined inaccurately

- an exclusion of any claims after too short a period, like 6 months for a project with a lifespan of decades

- an entire agreement or exclusive remedies clause which restricts rights and remedies to those expressly included in the appointment

- a clause requiring a party to notify the other of defects, issues or claims within a strict period (a condition precedent).

If you and your client do not understand what these terms mean it can spell disaster. If neither of you really knows what your limit is trying to achieve, you are not including terms which change behaviour, create trust or avoid disputes.

Interestingly, many of the limits on a contractor's liability under a standard form contract are in the form of remedies for breach such as limiting the contractor's liability for damages arising from delayed completion using delay damages [Chapter 10] or limiting the claims for defects by allowing the contractor to repair, replace or re-perform elements of the works.

Does It Really Matter?

Be Fair

A contractor on a house-building project in Hartlepool, limited its maximum total liability to the £250,000 contract price, despite having £1m of professional indemnity insurance cover.

The court had to consider if this was a fair and reasonable limit on its liability when its works were found to be defective.

> The court considered the bargaining position of the parties, the alternative contractors the client could have chosen, and the negotiations and concluded it was a fair and reasonable limit.[36]

Do You Need to Include Limits? No. If your small works contract says nothing, then a *time* limit is implied for bringing claims – known as the limitation period. Simple contracts have a limitation period of 6 years after completion of the initial works, whereas deeds have an extended limitation period of 12 years.[37] [Simple contract, deeds and limitation period are explained in the Glossary.]

There are some limits on the *amount* of any claim arising from breach of the terms of your small works contract. Your client can claim the damages that would put her in the position she would have been in had you properly performed the small works contract. She cannot recover losses which are not proven, too remote from the breach, or fanciful. The courts can also reduce the damages if there were other contributing factors, or the claim is unreasonable. In an infamous swimming pool case, Mr Forsyth's claim for £21,560 to rebuild his 'defective' swimming pool – it was too shallow – was rejected and he was awarded a mere £2,500 to reflect his disappointment in the finished, but useable, product.[38]

Why Should You Keep It Simple? Although all the terms in your small works contract should be written clearly, there are three factors specific to limits of liability:

1. **Limits affect the price.** You can take into account a simple limit on your liability when agreeing a suitable price for the works – the higher the limit, the higher your risk, and the higher your price could be.

2. **Limits are closely scrutinised by the courts.** If there is any contradiction or ambiguity, the courts will interpret them against you. If you write a limit which is uncertain the courts will throw it out!

3. **Limits are controlled by legislation.** For claims brought by a business client your limits have to be reasonable[39] and for claims brought by a consumer client, your limits have to be fair.[40] The wider and more complex your limit, the more likely the court will reject it as unreasonable.

How You Can Write It Simply: For defects, you can include a right for you to return and repair:

> We will make good without charge any defects which appear within <insert> months of completion.

For other breaches of contract, you can simply limit your liability to a specific sum:

> If we breach this contract, our total liability for any one claim, excluding claims arising from fraud, death or personal injury, will not exceed £<insert figure>.

Legislation means your limit must be at least your fees for consumer contracts.[41] It is very difficult to provide guidelines for a reasonable limit in a B2B small works contract as the court considers the whole of the contract as well as a large number of other factors in determining whether a specific limit is reasonable. The worst that can happen is that your limit is held unreasonable and you have unlimited liability.

17

REMEDIES TO HELP YOU AVOID THE COURTS

Your small works contract will create more trust and help you avoid formal disputes if it includes simple remedies when one party breaches its terms. Your contract should take a pragmatic approach and include ways to help you resolve common issues quickly.

Under the Consumer Rights Act 2015, if your client is a consumer, your small works contract must include a complaints procedure and a remedy allowing your client to ask you to re-perform any works that she is not completely satisfied with, or provide a (partial) refund.

Other common remedies for construction projects are:

■ Financial compensation for your client when the works are completed late, called delay damages [Chapter 10]

■ Grace periods for you when events outside your control delay completion, called extensions of time [Chapter 14]

■ A period during which you can repair or replace defective parts of the works, called a defects period [Chapter 16]

■ Remedies for late payment

■ Rights to end the contract early, cancellation or termination [Chapters 18 and 19]

■ Remedies for resolving disputes.

Avoiding Common Errors

The biggest mistake that contract writers make is not realising that each of these express contractual remedies helps to avoid the parties having to take a dispute to court. The remedies provide a quick-fix solution instead of one party having to prove:

- the existence of a relevant express or implied term,

- the other party has breached that term; i.e. they have not complied with it,

- that breach has caused them to incur costs or suffer losses, and

- the precise amount of those costs or losses which can be attributed to the breach.

All contractual remedies are far simpler, cheaper and quicker to use and rely on for both parties so they really are a win-win element in any contract. Your small works contract not only needs remedies, the parties need to use them.

Does It Really Matter?

Effective Remedies

Mr and Mrs Baxter appointed a firm of contractors under a standard form contract to carry out alterations and extensions to their home in Oxfordshire for roughly £35,000. Following completion the contractor agreed to repair any defects for a further 6 months (the defect period).

Defects did arise in the works but the clients did not tell the contractor during the defect period and only raised them when the contractor sued for its final payment (due at the end of the defect period).

The court held that the defect clause gave the clients *an express right to require the contractor to return, as well as to the contractor*

> *[itself] the right to return and repair the defect.*
>
> As the clients did not tell the contractor about the defects, they could not recover the full cost of getting another contractor to repair them. The clients *cannot recover more than the amount which it would have cost the contractor [itself] to remedy the defects.*[42]

CONSUMER-ONLY REMEDIES

Do You Need to Include Consumer Remedies? No. A consumer client is entitled to ask you to repeat works or services if they do not meet the minimum criteria for time and quality, or for a price reduction if that is impractical.[43]

Why Should You Keep It Simple? Although these remedies are implied, not all of them are well-known, so it is wise to write the relevant ones into your small works contract.

How You Can Write It Simply: For consumer clients, your small works contract can provide:

> We will re-perform any Works which were performed without reasonable skill and care without charge, within a reasonable time and without inconveniencing you. If repeat performance is not possible, we will refund up to <insert>% of the Price for those Works.

OTHER CONTRACTUAL REMEDIES

Do You Need to Include Remedies? No. There are three *implied* remedies that can help:

1. **Interest:** if your business client does not pay your invoices in full, your remedy is interest at 8% above the current base rate[44] (this can be added into consumer contracts using an express term).

2. **Suspension:** under a construction contract (i.e. for a business client whose project lasts more than 45 days), if your client does

not pay your invoices in full, and she has not issued a pay-less notice, you can suspend carrying out any or all of your works. [Chapter 11]

3. **Adjudication:** disputes on construction projects can be referred to a swift dispute resolution procedure called adjudication (if your client is a business this is mandatory[45]).

Why Should You Keep It Simple? It is far better to deal clearly and proactively with potential issues. It is better to set the ways you want to resolve disputes before you fall out (when it is hard to get anything agreed). Also, once goods, materials and works have been completed, they belong to the landowner and you cannot remove them; so you need to know what other remedies you have if your client does not pay.

How You Can Write It Simply: Although interest is not mandatory for consumer contracts, it acts as a useful nudge if your client is a recalcitrant payer. You can choose any rate of interest, which is often 5% above the base rate (although any other substantial alternative remedy can be used):

You will pay simple yearly interest at <insert>% on all overdue sums.

Although adjudication is not required for consumer contracts, it is a swift, simple and relatively cheap process that is useful as a first step:

If we cannot resolve a dispute amicably, either party can refer it to adjudication under the Scheme for Construction Contracts 1998/649 (amended), with <insert relevant body> nominating the adjudicator.

18

CANCELLING THE CONTRACT (NO FAULT)

There are three aspects to cancellation that your small works contract needs to consider:

- A cooling-off period [Glossary] for consumer contracts during which your client can cancel your contract without charge (this must be at least 14 days but can be longer).

- A right for your client to change her mind either before you have started to provide the works or afterwards, provided she pays compensation.

- A right for both parties to cancel future obligations under the contract when one of them is in breach/default, known as termination. [Chapter 19]

Avoiding Common Errors

If your client is a consumer, then your small works contract must include a right for your client to cancel your appointment for a short, cooling-off period.

Notwithstanding this, your client may believe she has a right to cancel your small works contract for other reasons – such as the project has gone over budget, she has lost faith in your competence, or she has got a better quote from another contractor.

This is not how contracts are meant to work. As legally-binding documents they create rights and obligations on both sides. Your contract grants you the right to provide all the works and requires your client to pay for all of them.

In practice, it would be stubborn and pig-headed to use your contract to force your client to continue with the works that she cannot afford or no longer wants. The flip side is that you do not want to encourage your client to treat your contract lightly and to enter into it frivolously knowing there is a free 'get out of jail' card. If she is going to have the right to end your contract early without cause, then she should have to pay for that privilege.

Does It Really Matter?

Calling It a Day: Does It Have To Be Reasonable?

In a long-term agreement with a Housing Association for the provision of works and services, a provider agreed to a term allowing cancellation without a good reason, also called 'termination for convenience'. The agreement also included a requirement for the parties to work together in *a spirit of trust, fairness and mutual co-operation*.

Following a review of the payments made, the Housing Association decided to cancel the contract – as allowed – by giving 3-months notice. The provider claimed compensation for future lost profits, totalling over £1m. The court held that the agreement allowed either side to *terminate for any or even no reason*. The decision did not have to be objectively reasonable.[46]

Where the client's decision has to be reasonable, motive can be important. In another case the court said that if the client decided to cancel the contract as part of an ulterior motive – such as harassing or annoying the provider – it would have acted unreasonably and in breach of the agreement.[47]

COOLING OFF

Do You Need To Include a Cooling-off Period? For a consumer client, you must allow your client to cancel your small works contract within 14 days (unless the contract is made on your premises). Your contract should also include a cancellation form, although your client is not obliged to use it.

The impact of these rules is that you should not start to provide the works before the end of the cooling-off period, unless your client specifically asks you to. If you do provide services during this period – at her request – then either:

- your client can still cancel your contract but has to pay for the value of any works provided, or

- your client cannot cancel if the works have already been provided in full before she decides to cancel.

If the services you are providing are low-value urgent repairs or maintenance then your client cannot cancel during the cooling-off period.

Why Should You Keep It Simple? If you do not include this right and relevant notice then you are not meeting your legal obligations under the Consumer Rights Act 2015.

How You Can Write It Simply: If your client is a consumer, it is critical for her right to cancel to be clear and simple:

You can cancel this contract up to 14 days after its date by sending this form or any other clear written notice.

Cancellation Form

To <insert contractor name, address and email>

We <insert client names, address and contact details> are cancelling the contract for <describe type of> works at < location>.

Date <insert>

CHANGING HER MIND

Do You Need To Include a Right To Change Her Mind? No. Your small works contract will still be legally binding and will entitle you to carry out all of the works.

Why Should You Keep It Simple? A right to cancel benefits your client, and helps build trust as it demonstrates that you recognise the collaborative nature of the contract. Once it is clear that you cannot work together, you should make it easy for both of you to end the contractual relationship as painlessly as possible.

Any right to cancel due to a change of mind (termination for convenience) should reflect and compensate you for the profit you won't earn by carrying out the remainder of the works.

How You Can Write It Simply: The right to cancel should set out when your client can cancel and the monies payable:

> You can cancel any of the Works by <insert> days' written notice provided you pay for all Works completed by the date of your notice (and we will invoice for any Works not previously invoiced) and £<insert> to compensate us for our lost profits on the cancelled Works.

When there are issues of fault or insolvency, then a better remedy for both parties is termination.

19

TERMINATING THE CONTRACT (PARTY FAULT)

You don't have to allow your client to end your right to finish the works early – you might think that the remedy in Chapter 18 is a step too far. If your client isn't 100% sure that she wants you to carry out all the works, perhaps she shouldn't enter into a contract with you at all!

However, your small works contract should give both you and your client a right to stop any future works if either party is in default or has breached the contract. As all construction projects rely on trust and collaboration [Chapter 13] once that trust has gone and it's turned into a sort of turf warfare, then it makes more sense to go your separate ways than continue.

Avoiding Common Errors

Termination is a key remedy. It is a serious step as it stops you carrying out the works you were contracted to perform. It should only apply when your relationship with your client has broken down irrevocably. Termination should not be used frivolously or to put pressure on the other party.

Your small works contract needs:

■ a mutual right to terminate

■ clarity around which trigger events will allow the parties to terminate

- a mechanism to notify the other party (written notice)

- a time period between the notice and when the works will end (best kept short)

- how outstanding payments will be dealt with.

Both parties should be allowed to terminate. Too often contracts only allow the paying party to bring the project to an end. But if your client will not co-operate, will not pay, is preventing you from doing your job or goes bust, it is better to stop the works, particularly as you are no longer working together ...

Does It Really Matter?

When The Project Grinds To a Halt

On a project for extensive refurbishment and alterations to a house in St Albans, the parties fell out. The clients claimed that progress was far too slow. The contractor struggled to get a list of outstanding works and defects and to get paid. The contractor suspended work because it did not want to work at risk of not getting existing or further monies.

The court held that the clients *were in breach of what to the claimant was a most important term of the contract, namely that reasonable sums due should be paid at reasonable intervals. Not only were the [clients] in breach of contract ... for not paying, they were threatening (in breach of contract) not to pay any further sums until the works were completed ... A refusal to honour payment obligations at least insofar as it relates to a relatively sizeable sum of money due or the threat not to pay further sums due in accordance with the contract must be capable of being [a breach allowing termination].*[48]

Do You Need To Include Termination? No. As noted, a contract creates both an obligation and a right for you to provide all the works and to get paid for them. Any right to stop those works before you have finished, should be limited to prevent canny clients chucking you off a project without a good reason.

It is entirely up to you how strictly you want to rely on your right to finish. For a consumer client, you have to give her a right to cancel the contract during the cooling-off period; and you may (but need not) give her a right to end the contract without default [Chapter 18].

You could rely on the implied right to terminate future obligations of your contract for *fundamental breaches*; i.e. acts which indicate a party no longer intends to comply with its duties under the contract. However interpreting whether the individual or cumulative acts of a party are sufficient to entitle you to terminate is highly technical and legally complex. Generally, you are under an obligation to prove that the other committed a fundamental breach; if not, you will be liable to pay damages to compensate the other for ending the contract without sufficient cause.

Why Should You Keep It Simple? A simple right to terminate without the need to *prove* that a party has committed a fundamental breach can help you avoid technical legal arguments or dispute resolution proceedings. However, as termination has serious consequences for both parties, there is still considerable scope for disputes to arise – not only is this aspect a legally complex area, but by this time you may have fallen out and there is less goodwill to broker a sensible settlement.

How You Can Write It Simply: Your remedy should leave neither party tempted to terminate for financial gain, but also neither worried about using the remedy when the circumstances are pointing inexorably to an irretrievable breakdown.

Your small works contract could say:

> If there is a serious breach of this contract either party can end the contract by giving <14> days' written notice to the other, or immediately for insolvency. After that notice period, we will leave the site clean and tidy, stop further works, and – unless we were in breach – invoice you a reasonable sum relating to any works not yet invoiced.

You could explain in your contract what types of serious breach you have in mind. You may want a right to terminate when your client stops paying or refuses to pay your invoices, prevents you carrying out the works; e.g. refusing access or not replying to requests for instructions. Your client may want to terminate if you are seriously incompetent, or abandon the works.

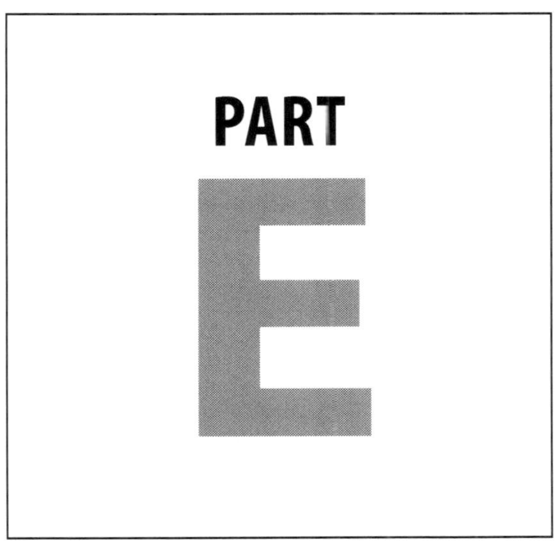

NEXT STEPS FOR CONTRACT SUCCESS

Once you've actioned Parts B, C and D in this book, you will have an outline or draft small works contract which contains the bare minimum, the client-centred content and a variety of effective extras. It will be simple, robust, and workable. You have also learnt how to plan a simple document that builds trust and avoids disputes.

You are now in control of your business, your works and your relationships with your clients.

Your outline 500-word small works contract, by itself, is not enough to create success. You need to be able to create client-specific contracts that you and your client can read and understand. You both also need to be able to use your small works contract properly. This means you need to:

- ask great questions to create your client-specific contract [Chapter 20]

- after it is sent, focus on negotiating only the showstoppers [Chapter 21] and check that your client really is happy with her role in the success of the project [Chapter 23]

- use your small works contract effectively – process is as important as content [Chapter 22]

- double-check you have understood all the guidance in this book [Chapter 24].

This Part will help you make small works contracts really effective for you.

20

CREATING A CLIENT-SPECIFIC CONTRACT

Although you now have the right content outline for your small works contract, you need to learn to tailor it to each client. A one-size-fits-all approach does not work for creating contracts for bespoke projects.

Your small works contract should record your precise agreement with your client for her project. The quality of your first draft is directly related to the quality of the questions you ask your client.

Each small works contract needs to be different to the last, so you need to modify:

1. The name and details for your client [Chapter 8]

2. The precise works required [Chapter 9]

3. When you expect to start and complete the works [Chapter 10]

4. The price to be paid and the way she will pay in instalments [Chapter 11]

5. The quality/performance you require [Chapter 12]

6. Your client's project-specific objectives [Chapter 13].

If you really want your small works contract to be client- and project-specific, you should carefully review every clause proposed in Part D before you send it to your potential client.

The Questions You Should Ask

Before you send the small works contract, ask yourself:

- What does your client *really* want to achieve (what does success look like)?

- Which of the key project aims (time, cost, quality or other) is the most important?

- How will your works help your client achieve her goals or solve her problems?

- What special aspects about your client and her project do you need to reflect in your contract?

- Are there specific procedures, risks or remedies that your contract needs to include?

- Does your contract explain what's unique about your business and is it in your tone of voice?

- Does your contract build trust?

- Will your client understand *why* they should work with you?

- Will your client know *how* to work with you?

Agree Before You Start Work

It is not enough to want to work together on a project, with a clear scope of works and agreed price. Other elements of your contract can be critical to one or both of the parties. A £1.68m project was completed and, because of a dispute, the courts spent 7 years and the parties spent a huge amount of money trying to work out what the terms of their contract were – nothing was ever signed!

The Supreme Court said *The different decisions in the courts below and the arguments in this court demonstrate the perils of beginning work without agreeing the precise basis upon which it is to be done. The moral of the story is to agree first and to start work later.*[49]

Once you have created a version of your small works contract for your client, she will need to read it carefully to check that it accurately records her understanding of your agreement. She may want to negotiate specific aspects. This requires give-and-take and for you to know how to negotiate what really matters to your company

90

21

NEGOTIATING YOUR SMALL WORKS CONTRACT

The purpose of creating a contract outline is to decide, before you get stuck into an individual project, how you want to work with your ideal clients. It is far too easy to get drawn into tasks, discussions and negotiations, ending up with a deal to which you would never have said *yes* to at the start.

The purpose of planning and crafting your small works contract is to have a good starting point, which you then refine to meet the needs of individual clients. As discussed, it should be a fair and balanced document to build trust and avoid disputes. Your job is to avoid including showstoppers which I define as

A clause or term that could bring negotiations or your contract to a juddering halt.

Not every client will accept your small works contract without asking for some changes. This book has provided the background to the clauses so you have more confidence to stick to what's important to you (your showstoppers). Additionally, you should negotiate your small works contract so that it suits both you and your client: win-win.

The key to negotiation is to know what you'd like in an ideal world and what you're prepared to concede. You need to decide your own showstoppers, but here are some clauses that you should consider very carefully:

Showstoppers

- Your client will not pay your price until the works are completed to her satisfaction. This could result in vexatious clients never paying a penny. If your client gets something of value from your works, such as a new extension, then you should get paid.

- No limit on your liability, or – even worse – a clause under which you indemnify your client for any losses arising from your works. You can't afford to surrender your business for one client so *always* limit your liability.

- Your client having a right to cancel the contract at any time *without* paying either your price for the works to date *or* compensation for works contracted for but no longer required/provided. This is a 'terminate for free' clause and is not advisable, except for the limited period (14 days) granted under consumer legislation. An alternative is in Chapter 18.

- Your client asking you to sell or assign your copyright in any documents, data or designs that you create. At most, your client needs an exclusive perpetual royalty-free licence. If you are preparing bespoke designs for a project, you should add a copyright licence to your small works contract. See Chapter 12 of 'How to Write Simple and Effective Consultant Appointments in Just 500 Words' for sample text.

- Your client having a right to deduct amounts from your payments without giving you a notice stating her reasons and calculating how her losses were caused by you.

Learn to Compromise

For any term which is not a showstopper, and these are personal, you need to decide the limit of your ability or desire to compromise. For each client you must decide your 'walk away position' before you become too involved – it's part of your business strategy and shows you value your own expertise. You can get another client to help 'fill your fridge', but a bad contract can leave you facing insolvency.

22

USE YOUR SMALL WORKS CONTRACT EFFECTIVELY

There are a number of unhelpful myths about using small works contracts:

Myth	Reality
You should not read a contract all the way through	You *should* if you want to avoid betting your business on a roll of some weighted dice
You should not query the terms in a contract	You *should* unless the terms have been written so they cannot possibly be misunderstood
You should not negotiate the terms of your small works contract	You *should* as you need to work *with* your client
You do not need to sign your contract	Although this is not strictly necessary [Chapter 3] it does ensure tidiness of process and prevents later arguments about whether it was actually agreed
Once signed, you should shove your contract in a drawer (or file electronically) and never refer to it	You *need* to refer to it regularly unless you have a photographic memory for all the contracts you have agreed with all the clients you are working with at any particular time
The only purposes of your contract are firstly to get the job and lastly to resolve any disputes; so these are the only times you need to read, understand and use it	No. Just no.

Your small works contract can and should be a guide that explains how you will work to solve your client's problems. You cannot achieve success if you can't remember what you promised to do or how you said you would work together.

Your small works contract legally obliges you to carry out your works and certain duties in a specific manner. It also sets out clear procedures to follow, many of which are linked to rights and remedies for you or your client. This is not mere 'dolling up' of what you always do. Your small works contract is the critical tool you should employ to build trust and avoid disputes. Although trust is often built at the start by the use of a simple effective contract, it is continued by following up on the promises you made in that small works contract. You can hardly meet those promises if you can't remember what they are!

An effective contract is one that the parties *do use*, which affects their behaviour, governs their conduct and controls their excesses. It can also nip disputes in the bud if you follow its procedures properly.

Please do not make the mistake of shoving your small works contract in a drawer (or electronic file) or allowing it to gather dust on a shelf.

Instead, as it is short and sweet, pin it to your noticeboard or electronic dashboard, and keep referring back to it. Keep communicating with your client about progress to their goals and how you have met aspects of their expectations. Keep your client updated with any surprises (nice and nasty) and be prepared to openly discuss any concerns she has as soon as they arise.

23

IS YOUR CLIENT HAPPY?

At the same time as you send your small works contract, you could also check whether your client understands the project and her role in paying for the works as well as you think she does. My Happiness Check is designed to avoid frustrations, mis-matched expectations and unwelcome surprises during the works and after completion. It focuses on a major cause of disputes; i.e. money!

I designed this after interviewing consumers who had worked with companies like yours and listening to the visceral negative feelings that discussing the construction process threw up. Many felt they had no choice but to continue when they really wanted to throw in the towel. Some would have sued if they could have afforded to. Many told their friends how bad contractors had made them feel.

Use this Happiness Check to start your projects on the right foot and ensure your clients give you a glowing endorsement once you finish.

HOW HAPPY WILL YOUR CLIENT BE?

If your client is a consumer, this quiz can help check whether you have agreed all relevant aspects with your client to avoid friction from money issues.

Price certainty at the start			
1. Original Price of the Works [Chapter 11] Does your client know the price of the works (including any tax) – assuming no changes during the project? **TIP:** *UK consumer contracts must be priced to include any VAT*	No ☹	Roughly 😐	Yes 🙂
2. Scope of the Works [Chapters 9 and 12] Does your contract describe the scope and quality your client wants; will she know when you have finished and what will be extras? **TIP:** *Ask questions to check what your client understands*	No ☹	I think so 😐	Yes 🙂
Certainty over the payment process			
3. Payments on Account [Chapter 17] Have you agreed how often you can ask your client for payments before completion (called payments on account or instalments)? **TIP:** *Your schedule can be based on time periods or stages of the build*	No ☹	I'm not sure 😐	Yes – it is clear 🙂
4. Time to Pay [Chapter 17] Have you agreed how long you client has to pay your invoice after she receives it – whether by cash or electronic funds transfer? **TIP:** *If nothing is agreed, then it would be a reasonable time (7 days)*	No ☹	I think so 😐	Yes – both are clear 🙂
5. Getting Payments [Chapter 20] Have you checked how long it will take your client to get cleared funds (from savings or her lender) so she can pay you? **TIP:** *Make sure your client has enough time to get the money to pay*	No ☹	Not yet 😐	Yes 🙂

Certainty over the payment process			
6. Processing Payments [Chapter 20] Is the time to get cleared funds (answer to Q5) less than the time your contract says she has to pay you (answer to Q4)? **TIP:** *Late payment causes friction; it can end in court proceedings*	No, more ☹	The same time 😐	Yes, less ☺
7. Sharing Information [Chapter 20] Have you agreed what information you will provide to substantiate the costs on your invoices for both the original scope and extras? **TIP:** *Agree the information your client wants/needs before works start*	No ☹	Not sure 😐	Yes (or not needed) ☺
Extras – price certainty as the project continues			
8. Agreeing Extras [Chapter 14] Have you agreed to tell your client about the impact of any extras (on the price payable and the completion date) before carrying them out? **TIP:** *Your client should say yes/no before you implement any extras*	No ☹	I think so 😐	Yes ☺
9. Costing Extras [Chapter 14] Have you agreed that you will provide a quote for and agree the extra costs for any extra works before carrying them out? **TIP:** *If your client won't agree costs, you can charge a reasonable sum*	No ☹	I think so 😐	Yes ☺
10. Final Cost of the Works [Chapter 20] Have you agreed that you will provide regular updates on the total price of the works? **TIP:** *Surprises on completion can prevent your client enjoying the works*	No ☹	I think so 😐	Yes ☺

98

24

MAKING SENSE OF IT ALL

Where the Happiness Check reviews the *financial* side of things, there are many other guidelines offered in this book which will ensure your small works contract makes sense.

Work through this Sense-Checklist, referring back to the appropriate chapter as needed.

Do You Have the Bare Minimum for a Contract	Y/N	Chapter
Can you tell who the parties are?		8
Do you understand precisely the scope of works?		9
Have You Added Client-Centred Content?		
Can you identify the start and completion dates for the works?		10
Can you work out how much you will be paid for the works?		11
Do you know the performance standards for the works?		12
Does your small works contract set out your client's aims for the works?		13
Is Your Small Works Contract Effective?		
Does your small works contract limit the extent of changes to the works?		14
Can you manage unexpected events and risks?		15
Does your small works contract limit your liability?		16

Is Your Small Works Contract Effective?	Y/N	Chapter
Does your small works contract include payment procedures that comply, where relevant, with the Construction Acts?		17
Does your consumer contract include remedies for late or poor performance?		17
Does your small works contract include a right to take disputes to adjudication?		17
Does your small works contract allow your client to deduct delay damages?		10
Does your small works contract allow your consumer client to cancel during the cooling-off period?		18
Does your small works contract include mutual rights to terminate?		19
Will You Use Your Small Works Contract Effectively?		
Is your small works contract client-specific?		20
Have you deleted or negotiated all showstoppers?		21
Have you pinned your contract to your noticeboard or electronic dashboard?		22
Is your client happy she understands how much it will or may cost?		23

If you can say *yes* to these questions then you are in the best possible position to use your 500-word small works contract effectively and create project success.

Like all contracts, your small works contract is a tool to help you do business. If you wouldn't use the wrong tool for a specific job at home, then you shouldn't use the wrong contract to do a specific job on your project.

Rather than recycle any old mix of clauses, take the time now to create your perfect tool for that job: a simple, robust and 500-word small works contract.

GLOSSARY

Adjudication	A short form of dispute resolution which is mandatory for B2B construction contracts, with a procedure lasting between 28 and 56 days from when the dispute is referred to adjudication to the adjudicator's award.
Contract Administrator	An independent person named in a contract (1) acts on behalf of the client and (2) applies procedures such as making decisions on granting an extension of time to complete the works, agreeing the valuation of works in contractor invoices, and stating whether the initial works meet the required quality standards. A contract administrator can be the difference between success and failure/disputes.
Cooling-Off Period	Consumer contracts are required under English/Welsh law to include a minimum 14-day period during which the consumer client can cancel the contract without penalty. See The Consumer Contracts (Information, Cancellation and Additional Charges) Regulations 2013. This is also known as a cancellation period.
Deed	A deed is a special form of contract. It must meet the five legal requirements for a contract and it must also (1) state that it is a deed somewhere in the document, (2) be signed as set out by law, and (3) be delivered. The liability of the parties will last for 12 years from completion of the works.
Delay Damages	Also known as liquidated damages (LDs) or liquidated and ascertained damages (LADs). These are a pre-agreed fixed sum per week (or day) payable to the client for every week (or day) that the works are delayed beyond the completion date. They provide a quick and easy remedy for the client and help keep the contractor on schedule.
Fixed Price Contract	Also colloquially known as lump sum. A contract where the price for the works is agreed in advance and this is the price that the client will pay, irrespective of how much it actually costs the contractor to carry out those works. The price can change if the works are varied or there are other events entitling the contractor to more money.

Pay-Less Notice	A notice required under the Construction Acts 1996 and 2009. The notice has to be given by the client (as the paying party) to the contractor by a specific date (as set out in the contract). The notice has to state the amount the client intends to pay and the basis on which that new figure has been calculated. The Pay-Less Notice is required if the client wants to pay less than the amount on the Payment Notice. If it is not given, or not given on time, the contractor is entitled to be paid the full amount on the Payment Notice.
Payment Notice	A notice required under the Construction Acts 1996 and 2009. The notice can be given by either the client or the contractor and states the amount the party believes is due under the contract and the basis on which that figure has been calculated.
Simple Contract	Also known as a contract 'under hand'. An agreement meeting the five legal requirements (Chapter 3) signed by authorised representatives of the listed parties. Contrast this with a deed. The liability of the parties will last for 6 years from completion of the works.

FOOTNOTES

1 This library contains a variety of sample contract patterns or models to inspire you to think outside a text document format. https://contract-design.iaccm.com/

2 The definition is set out in the Construction Acts 1996 and 2009 (the Housing Grants, Construction and Regeneration Act 1996 as amended by the Local Democracy, Economic Development and Construction Act 2009).

3 This applies if you are a trader; i.e. acting in the course of a business or trade (see s2(2)) and your client is acting outside the course of any business (see s2(3)).

4 Arcadis Global Disputes Reports 2019 available at https://www.arcadis.com/en/united-kingdom/our-perspectives/2019/june/global-construction-disputes-report-2019/

5 NBS National Construction Contracts and Law Report 2018 available at https://www.thenbs.com/knowledge/national-construction-contracts-and-law-report-2018

6 The Consumer Contracts (Information, Cancellation and Additional Charges) Regulations 2013. Note that you should not start providing works before the 14-day cancellation period has ended, unless your client specifically requests this.

7 Your trading name, geographical address and telephone number.

8 McGlinn v Waltham Contractors Ltd [2007] EWHC 149 (TCC), paragraphs 39 and 160.

9 In Globe Motors Inc v TRW Lucas Varity Electric Steering Ltd [2016] EWCA Civ 396 the Court of Appeal said that a clause requiring any variation to be in writing and signed did not prevent an oral variation of the contract binding the parties.

10 As set out in the Arcadis Global Disputes Reports (see note above).

11 More accurately, you can only contract with someone with the capacity to contract, which excludes minors (people under 18 years of age), with mental capacity (so excluding mentally ill people) and with companies acting within their powers.

12 MG Scaffolding (Oxford) Limited v Palmloch Limited [2019] EWHC 1787.

13 https://beta.companieshouse.gov.uk/

14 This was changed by the Contracts (Rights of Third Parties) Act 1999 and third parties can sue if the party does or purports to confer a benefit on him or his class of people. In practice many contracts expressly state that no third parties can sue under this Act.

15 As partnerships do not have a separate legal personality under English/Welsh law, you may need to take legal advice to ensure your contract accurately records the correct entity and is correctly signed.

16 The report is available at https://blog.iaccm.com/free-resources/ten-pitfalls-to-avoid-in-contracting

17 Hart Investments Ltd v Fidler [2006] EWHC 2857.

18 According to 2018 UK Industry Performance Report available at https://www.glenigan.com/market-analysis

19 See Co-operative Group (CWS) Ltd (formerly Co-operative Wholesale Society Ltd) v International Computers Ltd [2003] EWHC 1 where there was a dispute about whether the supplier had guaranteed delivery of software on a specific date.

20 HDK Ltd (t/a Unique Home) v Sunshine Ventures Ltd & Ors [2009] EWHC 2866.

21 Hick v Raymond & Reid [1893] AC 22. Lord Watson said that a reasonable time "has invariably been held to mean that the party upon whom it is incumbent duly fulfils his obligation, notwithstanding protracted delay, so long as such delay is attributable to causes beyond his control, and he has neither acted negligently nor unreasonably."

22 Leander Construction Limited v Mulalley and Company Limited [2011] EWHC 3449.

23 Gilbert-Ash (Northern) Ltd v Modern Engineering (Bristol) Ltd [1973] 3 WLR 421, House of Lords decision.

24 See e.g. NBS National Construction Contracts and Law Survey 2015 where between 50-75% of respondents said the pricing mechanism most often use for their projects was a lump sum or fixed price basis.

25 Price is not the same as cost – most contracts are priced on a combination of cost and profit.

26   IACCM (2018), Top 10 Most Negotiated Terms. Available to members at https://s3.eu-central-1.amazonaws.com/iaccmportal/resources/files/10243_iaccm-top-negotiated-terms-small-file.pdf

27   Clarke & Sons v Act Construction [2002] EWCA Civ 972.

28   Section 15 of the Supply of Goods and Services Act 1982 as replaced by Section 51(2) of the Consumer Rights Act 2015 (for service contracts with consumers).

29   Section 109(1) of the Housing Grants Construction and Regeneration Act 1996 (as amended). If your small works contract does not contain an agreement to pay by instalments then the relevant provisions of the Scheme for Construction Contracts 1998 SI 649 (as amended) will apply.

30   Trebor Bassett and Cadbury v ADT Fire and Security [2012] EWCA Civ 1158.

31   Bolam v Friern Hospital Management Committee [1957] 2 All ER 118.

32   Bingham LJ, Eckersley v Binnie & Partners [1988] 18 Con LR 1.

33   Eribo v Odinaya And Logicplough Property Ltd [2010] EWHC 301.

34   Abbey Developments Ltd v PP Brickwork Ltd [2003] EWHC 1987.

35   Independent Broadcasting Authority v EMI and BICC Construction [1995] PNLR 179, HL Lord Edmund-Davies.

36   Shepherd Homes Ltd v Encia Remediation Ltd [2007] EWHC 70.

37   Limitation Act 1980 ss5 and 8.

38   Ruxley Electronics and Construction Ltd v Forsyth [1995] UKHL 8.

39   Section 2(2) Unfair Contract Terms Act 1977 for B2B.

40   Fairness is based on considering whether a term causes a significant imbalance in the parties' rights and obligations, to the detriment of the consumer. Such terms will be deleted from your appointment and cannot bind a consumer client.

41   Under Section 49 of The Consumer Rights Act 2015, liability cannot be limited to less than the contract price.

42   Pearce & High Ltd v Baxter & Anor [1999] EWCA Civ 789.

43   If repeating your performance of the works would cause you significant inconvenience or is impossible, then your client is entitled to claim a price reduction of up to 100% of your fees, payable within 14 days of agreeing the refund. See Section 56 of the Consumer Rights Act 2015.

44   As required by the Late Payment of Commercial Debts (Interest) Act 1998 (as amended).

45   Under the Housing Grants, Construction and Regeneration Act 1996 (as amended) and associated Schemes.

46   TSG Building Services plc v South Anglia Housing Ltd [2013] EWHC 1151.

47   Reinwood Limited v L Brown and Sons [2008] UKHL 12 gives six principles to help assess whether a party has acted unreasonably or vexatiously in terminating or cancelling a contract.

48   CJ Elvin Building Services Ltd v Noble & Anor [2003] EWHC 837, paragraphs 90 and 91.

49   RTS Flexible Systems Ltd v Molkerei Alois Müller GmbH & Co KG [2010] UKSC 38.

ABOUT THE AUTHOR

Sarah Fox has spent 25 years reading, analysing, critiquing, writing and training others on using construction contracts. At Eversheds LLP, she wrote, adapted, amended, negotiated and resolved disputes on contracts from 1 page to 100 pages.

She now specialises in helping construction professionals to build simple contracts. With JCT MW 2016 (a standard form contract for minor works, the most popular single standard form in UK construction) weighing in at over 25,000 words – unamended – the simplicity of writing 500-word contracts has become Sarah's personal project.

Simple means short, readable, understandable and usable. 500 words is roughly a single A4-page. Her contracts are elegant, clear and brief, and – most importantly – legally robust.

With this book as your guide, you can create simple small works contracts. To get additional support, readers can sign up for Sarah's emailed regular contract tips, download a small works contract template and get access to a host of handy resources for contractors.

Sarah is an award-winning keynote speaker and is an expert in simplifying contracts and contracting, making your agreements easier to read, understand and use. This is the fourth book in her series, which already covers writing simple and effective letters of intent, consultant appointments and collateral warranties ... all in just 500 words.

www.500words.co.uk

sarah@500words.co.uk

A THANK YOU CARD

This book was written during the lockdown period in 2020 caused by the global Covid-19 pandemic. In a period of huge uncertainty, I wanted something positive to focus on, so decided to write book 4 in my series.

The lockdown period was made bearable by thousands of tiny acts and many people. I want to thank just a few of them ... two fabulous speakers, communicators and business-women, Rowena and Lorna (to whom this book is dedicated), went on a weekend to Guernsey with me immediately before lockdown. The memories of that little slice of heaven and our moments of madness sustained me when cabin fever set in!

Gareth Malone set up a Great British Home Choir and his 50 rehearsals at 17:30 each weekday evening helped draw my working day to a firm close, preventing work overwhelming me and giving me something positive to lift my spirits. Rowena invited me to on-line training sessions with Steve Pullen, a judo coach, which helped me move beyond just my solo daily running and be sociable while getting sweaty, strong and supple. Learning new things just about kept me sane (even if sanity is over-rated).

Perhaps what gave me most joy was either my garden or the 1000km Brian and I did on our tandem across Cheshire and neighbouring counties. We might have missed the Bishop's Castle World Tandem Triathlon 2020, but we'll be ready for 2021!

If you have passed me on my runs, walks or cycles during lockdown and smiled, nodded, or said hello, thank you. If you have helped, nursed or cared for others, delivered my milk, veg or goods, emptied my bins, mended our roads or simply kept your country going during this time, thank you from the bottom of my heart.

Made in the USA
Middletown, DE
15 January 2022